Tucson Hiking Guide

TUCSON

HIKING GUIDE

Second Edition

Betty Leavengood

PRUETT PUBLISHING COMPANY
BOULDER, COLORADO

Printed in the United States
06 05 04 03 02   5

Library of Congress Cataloging-in-Publication Data

Leavengood, Betty, 1939–

    Tucson hiking guide / Betty Leavengood. — 2nd ed.
      p.   cm.
    Includes bibliographical references (p.) and index.
    ISBN 0-87108-865-7 (pbk.)
    1. Hiking—Arizona—Tucson Region—Guide-books. 2. Hiking—Arizona—Tucson Region—Safety Measures. 3. Tucson Region—Guidebooks. I. Title.
    GV199.42.A72T835   1997
    917.91'776—dc21   97-1805
                                             CIP

Cover and book design by Kathleen McAffrey, Starr Design
Book composition by Lyn Chaffee
Cover photograph by Betty Leavengood

Contents

The Santa Rita Mountains

Preface

In the spring of 1989, I wandered across ridges, through shindaggers and catclaw, into arroyos and over boulders, looking for Little Wild Horse Tank, where someone years before had put a few goldfish. "The fish are huge now," I told my son and a friend, my companions on this trek. "Wait until you see them." It turned out to be a long wait. Three hours of wandering and the goldfish were nowhere in sight.

When we finally found the goldfish, I vowed to re-hike the route and write the definitive guide to Little Wild Horse Tank. I did, and that description, plus thirty-two other descriptions, became the *Tucson Hiking Guide,* first published in 1991.

A lot has changed since then. The goldfish are gone, removed by the Forest Service, because they were not native. Little Wild Horse Tank is gone, filled by heavy rains that brought tons of sand and gravel rushing down the canyon. Trails that crossed private land have been rerouted. Fire has drastically changed the look of other trails. In short, it's time for a second edition.

I have re-hiked every trail in the original guide at least once and changed the descriptions accordingly. There are many changes. Ventana Canyon Trail now begins in the employees' parking lot of Ventana Canyon Resort. Esperero Trail has been rerouted to avoid a section of private land. Several new trailhead parking areas have been constructed. I've eliminated from this edition any trail that required bushwhacking or four-wheel-drive to get to the trailhead and added several new trails. For each trail I've included a map and a trail profile. Many of the pictures are new.

There's even a new cover. The cover of the first edition featured my husband, hiking off into the saguaros in his tennis shoes. I took this staged shot at the end of a roll and was surprised to find it on the cover. He never hikes or does any other exercise for that matter. He's endured merciless razzing from friends and coworkers, and his only request when I began working on this second edition was, "Get me off the cover!"

Although there are many changes, this edition remains a guide for the "Sunday hiker." Years ago, my parents and I would often go for a Sunday drive. We'd stop on a whim, walk around the lake, visit a relative, or get a Dairy Queen. So it is with the Sunday hiker. They start up the trail at a leisurely pace, stopping on a whim to inspect a packrat's nest or take in the view. Maybe they come upon an old foundation and wonder who built it, or they may ask, "Why is this trail named Pontatoc?"

If you are a Sunday hiker, this is the guide for you. You'll find detailed instructions to the trailhead from the intersection of Speedway Boulevard and Campbell Avenue. Once on the trail, you'll find the directions are specific. I, never having been too familiar with a compass, say turn "left or right" instead of "east or west." I include lots of history. If there's a foundation, as on the Cactus Forest Trail, I'll tell you why it's there, and I've tried to determine the reason for the names of all the trails.

In this second edition, I've been helped by many people. Linda Tuck added some valuable history about the Rincons. My daughter, Cheryl Graham, turned my rough drafts into readable trail profiles. Many friends—especially Ruth Butera, Jo Haslett, and Linda Cross—have helped me re-hike the trails and correct confusing sections. Because of their efforts, the directions are clearer.

Introduction

Tucson is a "hiker's heaven." To the north is the mountain range that dominates the Tucson skyline, the Santa Catalina range. Due east are the Rincons. Forty miles south of town are the Santa Rita Mountains. The Tucson Mountains to the west are the backdrop for our dramatic sunsets. Hiking is possible year round—the mild winters allow hiking in the lower elevations, and, in summer, the trails of the high mountains beckon.

To enjoy hiking in these mountains, you must be properly prepared and be aware of the hazards of hiking in this area. Too much exposure to the sun is dangerous. Not carrying enough water can result in serious illness or death. There are venomous creatures out there, such as rattlesnakes, scorpions, and Gila monsters. Cactus, amole, catclaw, and other thorny plants seem determined to attack you. Weather conditions can change quickly—what started out as a beautiful morning can become a storm by early afternoon.

Sounds bad! If you are properly prepared and aware of the dangers that exist, the chances of anything happening to you are remote. It is beautiful out there, and the only way you can see it is on your feet. Within a 45-mile radius of Tucson, the elevations go from 2,500 feet to nearly 10,000 feet. Vegetation changes from cactus to oak to ponderosa pine and Douglas fir. You may spot a javelina, coyote, deer, bighorn sheep, or in the highest elevations, even a bear. Hidden pools invite swimming on a hot day. The views extend seemingly forever or are limited by stark canyon walls.

This guide is intended to prepare you to hike in these mountains. The first chapter will discuss proper equipment and clothing for hiking here. The second chapter discusses what you should be aware of, such as too much sun, too little water, and those poisonous creatures. The rest of the guide is devoted to providing detailed descriptions of trails and is organized by mountain range.

Each hike is preceded by a box of information as follows:

General Description: a short description of the hike.
Difficulty: I used four categories—"easy" is a hike with minimum elevation gain or loss that nearly anyone could achieve; "moderate" is a

little harder, usually over 1,000 feet in elevation gain and over 3 miles one way; "difficult" has areas of steep elevation gain and will require most of the day; "extremely difficult" is a category that is limited to a few hikes in this guide. They require a long day, are usually over 5 miles one way, and are steep. **Best Time of Year to Hike:** exactly what it says. **Length:** Distance given is round-trip, unless it is a loop hike, then the distance refers to the entire loop. **Trail Profiles:** indicate the elevation gain on the trail. **Miles to Trailhead from Speedway/Campbell Intersection:** This is a major well-known intersection in Tucson. Finally, **Directions to Trailhead from Speedway/Campbell Intersection:** Specific directions are given from this intersection and can be adapted from any place in town. All hikes in this guide are on trails and all can be reached by passenger car.

Although I have made every effort to ensure the accuracy of the directions, you must take the final responsibility for translating that information to your vehicle and hiking boots. A government agency may change a trailhead or a street name. Heavy rains can wash out a section of a trail, or what appears to me as a distinctive landmark may mean nothing to you. Always carry this guide, a map of the area you are hiking, and a compass. Never, never hike alone. Do not overestimate your hiking ability and do not hesitate to turn back if you become disoriented. It is better to try again another day than to become the topic of a story on the evening news.

If you want further information concerning trails and trailheads or governmental policies, the following is a list of government agencies:

Coronado National Forest—(520) 670-4552

Coronado National Forest—Nogales Ranger District—(520) 281-2296

Coronado National Forest—Santa Catalina Ranger District—(520) 749-8700

Saguaro National Park—East District Visitor Center—(520) 733-5153

Saguaro National Park—West District Visitor Center—(520) 733-5158

Tucson Mountain Park—(520) 791-4873

Pima County Parks and Recreation—(520) 740-2690

Getting Ready

Shoes. Most of the trails in the Tucson area are rocky and steep, making a sturdy hiking boot with ankle support a must. Many styles are available from all-leather to a combination of leather and fabric. Without comfortable boots, hiking can be extremely unpleasant.

Socks. Wear two pairs—a thin inner pair and an outer pair of wool or wool/cotton blend.

Clothing. Wear layers. A cotton T-shirt, a lightweight long-sleeved cotton shirt, and a sweater or sweatshirt are good to start with. Lightweight long pants protect your legs from the thorny vegetation. Many hikes in this area start at a low elevation and climb several thousand feet, requiring more clothing at the top than at the beginning of the hike. Layering makes it possible to be comfortable at any elevation.

Hat. Wear a hat for protection from the sun. Many styles are available. I prefer a cotton hat with a wide brim that can be tossed in the washer after a few wearings.

Walking Stick. In the rough terrain around Tucson, a walking stick is helpful. Many styles are available for purchase, or you can make one of your own. I have seen several strong sticks made out of agave stalks, with rubber tips on the ends to prevent splitting.

Daypack. Many styles are available. I prefer a daypack with several pockets large enough to hold some permanent supplies. Keep a first-aid kit, knife, compass, lightweight poncho, sunscreen, aspirin, and insect repellent tucked away in one pocket of the daypack. There should be room for extra bottles of water, plenty of food, and a warm jacket.

Canteen. Many types of canteens are available. Whatever style you select, make sure that it is easy to get at while you're hiking. I prefer a bottle holder that fits a belt. You'll need extra water bottles to carry in your daypack. You can also purchase all sizes and shapes of water bottles at outdoor stores.

Map. Although there are individual trail maps included in this guide, an overall map of the mountain range is helpful. United States Geological Survey Maps are available for each range. The Southern Arizona Hiking Club has published hiking maps of the Santa Catalina, Rincon, and Santa Rita Mountains that are helpful.

Cell Phone. The number of rescues by the local search and rescue organization have been greatly reduced by hikers carrying cell phones. Often a rescue is initiated when the missing hiker is just late. By having a cell phone, the rescue is avoided by a call. Also in case of an emergency, a cell phone can be used to seek help. I have made calls from high points in all the mountain ranges in this book.

Hazards of Hiking Around Tucson

Hiking in the mountains around Tucson presents a hiker with several unique situations. The sun is intense; water is scarce; venomous creatures abound; the newly discovered hantavirus strikes victims quickly; Africanized "killer" bees are aggressive when disturbed; lightning strikes here are higher than in any other place in the United States, with the exception of an area near Naples, Florida; and, yes, it is totally possible to get hypothermia while hiking in the desert.

Sun. The sun shines here 360 days a year, according to the chamber of commerce. It's great for hiking and not so great for the skin.

The University of Arizona Cancer Center sponsors a Sun Awareness Project to make Tucsonans aware of the dangers of too much exposure to the sun. According to Paola Villar Werstler, health educator for the project, Tucson has the highest incidence of skin cancer of any place in the world, with the exception of Queensland, Australia. "Unfortunately," Villar Werstler explained, "for many years the idea that a tanned skin was healthy led to excessive exposure. Now we are seeing a dramatic increase in the incidence of skin cancer as a result. A tan is the skin's response to damage from UV rays."

Skin cancer is caused by the ultraviolet rays of the sun. Many geographic and meteorologic factors in southern Arizona combine to allow high intensities of ultraviolet radiation to reach the earth's surface. These factors include Tucson's 32 degree north latitude, 2,410-foot altitude, high number of clear days, high annual percentage of sunlight, and a high average daily temperature that encourages outdoor activity.

Despite the danger of skin cancer, it is possible to hike safely in the sun. The cardinal rule to remember is *never* hike in the Tucson area without a sunscreen that has a sun protection factor (SPF) of at least fifteen. Sunscreens block the ultraviolet rays. The higher the rating, the longer the rays are blocked. To see how effective your sunscreen is, check the "Sun Intensity Prediction" chart, which is published daily in both Tucson newspapers. The predictions given are for untanned Caucasians, assume there are no clouds, and indicate the number of minutes of exposure to the sun required to redden the skin at various times during the day. The intensity varies from sixteen minutes at noon in the summer to thirty minutes at noon during the winter months. For example, if you plan to be in the sun in July at noon, it would only take sixteen minutes for your skin to redden. A sunscreen with an SPF of fifteen would lengthen the time that you could safely be exposed to the sun. A good formula to use is the "times ten" rule. For instance, an SPF of 15 will protect 15 x 10, or 150 minutes (2-1/2 hours).

Many sunscreens are available. A few have an SPF as high as thirty-four. Several are water resistant. Follow the instructions for use that are on the product, which basically include applying the sunscreen thirty minutes before exposure and reapplying it after swimming or heavy perspiration. Experiment and see which product suits your skin best. Today's sunscreens are like fine lotions and have no medicinal odor.

In addition to sunscreen, the hiker should wear a wide-brimmed hat, a long-sleeved cotton shirt, and lightweight long pants. Sunglasses that screen ultraviolet rays are a necessity. It is best, although usually not practical when hiking, to avoid exposure to the sun between 10 A.M. and 3 P.M. In the summer, hiking should be confined to the higher elevations, because of the intensity of the sun and the extreme heat at lower levels.

If you would like more detailed information or advice on a particular sunscreen product, contact the Arizona Cancer Center at (520) 626-7935.

Water. Water is so important in Arizona that many statutes regulate its consumption and use. Each summer newspapers carry accounts of death and near death from lack of water. At the least, too little water can cause headache, nausea, cramps, and fatigue. Although water consumption is especially important in summer, because of the low humidity, adequate intake is important in all seasons.

Kevin Kregel, professor of Exercise Science at the University of Iowa, researched the effects of heat stress on the thermoregulatory and cardiovascular responses, or, in layman's terms, "what happens if you don't get enough to drink."

Kregel recommends that hikers pre-hydrate by drinking 20 ounces of fluid two hours before hiking. During the hike, they should take a good drink every fifteen minutes. Kregel warns, "By the time you feel thirsty, you are already slightly dehydrated." For hikes of long duration, Kregel recommends drinking a fluid-replacement beverage such as Gatorade. Avoid soda pop, fruit juices, caffeinated drinks, and alcoholic beverages—all act as diuretics and cause dehydration.

One bit of good news! The idea that hikers shouldn't drink cold water is no longer accepted. According to Kregel, current research shows that cold water is absorbed into the body quicker. In fact, Kregel recommends what I have been doing for years—"Freeze it!"

Venomous Creatures. Venomous creatures—snakes, scorpions, and Gila monsters—are prevalent in the Sonoran Desert and mountains around Tucson.

Arizona reportedly has more rattlesnakes than any other state. Regardless of who's counting, Arizona rattlers have the best press agent! Rarely is there a Western made without a coiled rattler in the center of the trail. The horse rears, our hero pulls his gun and shoots the snake between the eyes, thus averting certain disaster. In reality, rattlers present little threat to riders or hikers.

True, rattlers thrive in the canyons and mountains around Tucson. Of the eleven species of rattlers, the western diamondback is the most common, and the one you are most likely to see while hiking. The western diamondback is brownish-gray with diamond-shaped markings. It has a broad triangular head, and at the end of its tail is a "rattle"—a series of connected bony segments, which, when vibrated, make a sound similar to a baby's rattle.

Nancy Mellor, Registered Pharmacist and Poison Information Specialist for the Arizona Poison Control Center, reports that the Poison Control Center receives an average of two hundred calls a year regarding rattlesnake bites in Arizona. The majority of bites, according to Mellor, are "illegitimate"—that is, incurred while someone, usually a fifteen- to twenty-five-year-old male, is playing with the snake. Many of these bites happen when people are drinking, leading the staff of the Poison Control Center to say "snakes are attracted to alcohol!" "Legitimate" bites, those suffered accidentally, are rare, although their number has increased in recent years.

While hiking, observe a few simple precautions. Since most bites happen to the extremities, do not put your hands or feet under a rock or log or anyplace else a snake might be sleeping. Never sit down without looking. Wear sturdy hiking boots that cannot be penetrated by fangs and long pants that will hinder the effect of a bite. If you see a snake, assume that it is poisonous and give it a wide berth. If you hear a rattle, stop immediately, determine the location of the snake, and get away from it.

If you or someone in your hiking party should be bitten, the single most important thing you can do, according to Mellor, is to remain calm and seek medical care. She adds, "Your best defense is your car keys."

Some specialists are beginning to cautiously recommend use of *Sawyer's First-Aid Kit—The Extractor,* an inexpensive device that uses a vacuum suction to extract venom. Mellor advises that the kit must be used immediately after the bite occurs and that the cup that catches the blood must be continuously emptied. She added that the Poison Control Center is not yet officially recommending the use of the kit until more studies have been conducted.

The center does recommend applying a wide constricting band between the bite and the heart, *making sure that the band is loose enough so that a finger can be inserted between it and the limb. Complications can occur with an improperly applied band.* Also, if possible, immobilize the limb with a splint or a sling.

Until recently, experts recommended cutting across the bite and sucking the venom out. Mellor advises *never* to cut a snake bite. More damage can be caused by the cut than by the actual bite. Other don'ts include: don't apply ice to the bite area; don't give the victim alcohol; and don't waste time catching the snake, because today's antivenins are effective against the bites of all pit vipers, regardless of their kind.

Scorpions also unnecessarily strike fear into the hearts of hikers. Of the thirty species of scorpions in Arizona, only one, the bark scorpion, is poisonous. Although chances of a fatality from a scorpion bite are remote (no deaths have occurred in Arizona in thirty years), caution should nevertheless be observed. Scorpions spend the daylight hours under cover and only emerge at night, and then, only when the nighttime lows exceed 77 degrees Fahrenheit. The bark scorpion never burrows and is most commonly found in riparian areas, such as in desert canyons and in groves of mesquite, cottonwood, and Arizona sycamore. The bark scorpion is most likely to bite when disturbed by a hiker leaning on a tree or moving a log. Although the bark scorpion can be distinguished from other species, any scorpion bite should be taken seriously. If possible, capture the scorpion so it can be determined if it is a bark scorpion.

The best first-aid treatment for a scorpion bite is to get to a medical facility as soon as possible. If you cannot reach medical assistance within thirty minutes, apply a loose constricting band between the sting and the heart.

The Gila monster also has a good press agent. The Gila monster is a brilliantly colored black and yellow or black and pink creature, so rare that it is protected by Arizona state law. Legend has it that once a Gila monster bites, it will not release its victim until thunder is heard. Although Gila monsters are the only lizard in the United States whose bite is poisonous, danger to hikers from Gila monsters is negligible. They are rarely seen in the wild. If one is seen at all, it will most likely be at dusk or after a summer rain in a canyon bottom, where the lizard has access to moist soil. To get bitten by a Gila monster while hiking, you would practically have to fall near one and surprise it. The overwhelming majority of bites have occurred to people handling captive Gila monsters.

Should you or a member of your party get bitten by a Gila monster, you don't have to wait until it thunders. A Gila monster will, however, hold on for at least fifteen minutes, during which time venom is pouring into the wound. The first thing to do is to get the Gila monster to release its grasp so as to limit the amount of venom that is injected into the body. A strong stick between the jaws usually works. If the stick is ineffective, the Gila monster may be encouraged to release its grip if you place an open flame under its jaw. Immersing the wounded extremity and the Gila monster under water might also work. If neither a stick, flame, nor water is available, grab the Gila monster by the tail and jerk. This will cause more damage to the wound, but anything is better than letting the Gila monster retain its grip.

First aid for a Gila monster bite involves letting the wound bleed freely for several minutes, while you flush it with water. Apply a loose constricting band between the wound and the heart. Immobilize the limb and seek medical help as soon as possible.

Further information and advice is available twenty-four hours a day from the Arizona Poison Control Center. In Tucson call 626-6016. Outside of the Tucson calling area, call 1-800-362-0101.

Hantavirus. This recently discovered deadly disease is thought to be transmitted when humans inhale particles of dried rodent urine and feces. Hikers should avoid contact with rodent-infested structures, such as abandoned cabins. All food should be carried in rodent-proof containers, and care should be taken to avoid rodent burrows.

Lightning. Lightning can be deadly in the mountains surrounding the city. Summer monsoon storms come up quickly and you need to take precautions when they do. Get off peaks, cliffs, and the ends of ridges. If you are in the forest, try to find a clump of trees shorter than the surrounding trees. Toss anything metal, such as a drinking cup or metal hiking stick, far away from you. If you are caught out in the open, squat on the ground and rest your head on your knees. Do not lie on the ground or get in a drainage ditch. Deep caves are safe, but stay away from shallow rock overhangs. Finally, if you are in a group, keep at least 50 feet apart to reduce the chance of everyone being struck. If someone in your party is struck by lightning, immediately begin CPR and seek medical assistance.

Hypothermia. Hypothermia, the lowering of the body's core temperature, is generally thought of as a condition that occurs in higher elevations than exist around Tucson. However, sudden changes in weather conditions here, especially atop the mountain ranges, can bring on cold rain or snow and cause the body temperature to fall to dangerous levels. Symptoms of hypothermia include drowsiness, uncontrollable shivering, impaired judgement, and weakness. Often victims do not realize that they are developing hypothermia, thus, it is always best to hike with a companion. The best treatment for hypothermia is to avoid it in the first place. Layer clothing and always keep rain gear, such as an inexpensive, lightweight poncho, in your daypack. Carry extra high-energy bars and always drink plenty of liquid. Should someone in your party develop hypothermia, immediately replace wet clothing with dry. Huddle with the person to help transfer warmth to their body, give warm liquids if possible, and seek medical assistance as soon as possible. Hypothermia can be deadly.

Africanized Bees. African bees were brought to South America to help increase honey production. In 1957 these bees began moving north, reaching Arizona in 1993. They are nicknamed "killer bees" because they are far more aggressive than other bees. Humans and animals have died in Arizona from Africanized bee attacks. The Arizona Department of Agriculture Africanized Honey Bee Advisory Committee advises wearing light-colored clothing while hiking and avoiding all scented products. If attacked, run as far and as fast as possible, preferably into brush. If you are stung, seek medical attention.

All this sounds formidable. Don't let it deter you from hiking and enjoying the out-of-doors. Just be aware of the dangers that exist and be prepared for emergencies.

Trail Difficulty Ratings

What follows is a totally unscientific rating of the trails in this guide, dividing them into four categories: *Extremely Difficult* trails are long, steep, tortuous climbs into the high country that should be attempted only by experienced hikers. *Difficult* trails are fairly long, but occasionally short and very steep, which, although difficult, don't have that built-in torture factor characteristic of the extremely difficult category. *Moderate* trails are pleasant hikes with some climbing, but not enough to really strain your muscles. *Easy* trails are rambles that anyone can do.

Extremely Difficult

Trail	Mountain Range	Page
Rincon Peak	Rincons	93
Esperero Trail	Santa Catalinas	111
Ventana Canyon	Santa Catalinas	117
Finger Rock	Santa Catalinas	128
Pima Canyon	Santa Catalinas	134
Old Baldy Trail	Santa Ritas	165

Difficult

Trail	Mountain Range	Page
Tanque Verde Ridge	Rincons	82
Douglas Spring Trail	Rincons	88
Box Camp Trail	Santa Catalinas	157
Super Trail	Santa Ritas	172
Agua Caliente Loop	Santa Ritas	186
Agua Caliente Trail	Santa Ritas	197
Florida Saddle Trail	Santa Ritas	200

Moderate

Trail	Mountain Range	Page
Hugh Norris Trail	Tucson Mountains	16
King Canyon	Tucson Mountains	22
Sendero Esperanza Trail	Tucson Mountains	27
Sweetwater Trail	Tucson Mountains	32
David Yetman Trail	Tucson Mountains	36
Brown Mountain	Tucson Mountains	57
Pink Hill	Rincons	75
Sabino to Hutch's Pool	Santa Catalinas	101
Blackett's Ridge	Santa Catalinas	106
Pontatoc Ridge	Santa Catalinas	123
Romero Canyon	Santa Catalinas	140
Prison Camp	Santa Catalinas	145
Butterfly Trail	Santa Catalinas	151
Kent/Bog Springs	Santa Ritas	177
Dutch John Spring Trail	Santa Ritas	182
Elephant Head Trail Hike/Bike	Santa Ritas	191

Easy

Trail	Mountain Range	Page
Golden Gate Loop	Tucson Mountains	41
Kinney Road Access	Tucson Mountains	47
Starr Pass	Tucson Mountains	52
Gilbert Ray Loop	Tucson Mountains	62
Cactus Forest Trail	Rincons	70

THE TUCSON MOUNTAINS

Tucson's sunsets are one of our city's trademarks. The mountains silhouetted on postcards are the Tucson Mountains, the smallest of the four ranges that surround Tucson. The high point, Wasson Peak at 4,687 feet, is barely a mountain by most standards.

The Tucson Mountains are different in character from the other ranges. No ponderosa pines will shade your path while you are hiking here. This is the land of mesquite and palo verde, of the saguaro, prickly pear, cholla, and hedgehog cacti, of creosote bushes, ocotillo, and catclaw. The terrain is a jumble of boulders and craggy ridges.

From A.D. 900 to 1300, the Hohokam lived in the river bottoms in their pit houses and hunted in the Tucson Mountains. Petroglyphs in King Canyon and Picture Rocks remain as evidence of the Hohokam's existence. The Hohokam were gone when the Jesuit priest, Father Kino, first came to the Tucson area in 1692. By then, the Pima were living at the base of the mountain we now call Sentinel Peak, or "A" Mountain.

The Tucson Mountains were significant in the early history of Tucson. When in 1772, King Carlos II of Spain, who possessed this land on paper, issued an order calling for the reorganization of the presidios (forts) in Mexico and the Southwest, the site selected was a point near the Santa Cruz River opposite the Pima village. Here, beginning in 1776, a new presidio was to be built. Progress was slow, and it was not until December 1783 that the task was completed. A lookout was maintained on top of Sentinel Peak, and the fort was warned when the Apaches swept down out of the Santa Catalinas or the Rincons. Several attacks were withstood, and the Royal Presidio of San Agustin del Tucson outgrew the walls of the fort by the mid-1800s. Sentinel Peak was no longer needed as a lookout.

The mountain did serve other purposes. Many early Tucson homes and the wall around the University of Arizona were built from black rock quarried from the side of Sentinel Peak. Today, a huge, white "A" representing the University of Arizona dominates the peak.

Copper was discovered in the 1870s at Silver Bell, and mining became important. Hikers in the Tucson Mountains today can see much evidence of early mining. The Sendero Esperanza Trail passes the old Gould Mine, once thought to be the bonanza of the territory. The Hugh Norris Trail passes several mines. The Starr Pass Trail follows the route of a shortcut through the mountains to the mines of Quijotoa.

As late as the 1920s and 1930s the land in the Tucson Mountains was open to homesteading. A stone house remains on the David Yetman Trail that was homesteaded in 1930 by a newspaper man from Illinois. Ranchers ran cattle in the mountains.

It seemed that the Tucson Mountains were open for grabs. Mining, cattle grazing, and homesteading were being carried on with little regard for the ecology of the mountains, until Pima County agricultural agent C. B. Brown took it upon himself to preserve the Tucson Mountain area. With the help of Senator Carl Hayden, Brown was able to persuade Congress to withdraw 60,000 acres from the Homesteading Act of 1873 to be used as Tucson Mountain Park.

World War I veterans complained that their rights were being violated because they could not homestead, and, as a result, all but 28,988 acres were turned back over to the United States Department of Interior to be used for homesteading. On April 11, 1929, the remaining acreage was designated as Tucson Mountain Park. The Pima County Parks Commission was established, and Brown was named chairman.

In 1933, part of the land designated for homesteading became part of Saguaro National Monument. In 1994, the designation was changed to Saguaro National Park.

The area was still not pristine and secure from development. Mining was still permitted on much of the land. In 1939 Columbia Pictures leased 300 acres of state land that was within the park for movie production and built Old Tucson. In one scene, 6 acres of desert were set on fire, completely destroying all vegetation, including several mature saguaros. Public uproar caused the Pima County Park Commission to purchase the lease from Columbia Pictures, ensuring control and that no fires would be set in the desert again.

In 1952, Arthur Pack, a member of the park commission, recommended a living museum be established in Tucson Mountain Park to educate the public about the Sonoran Desert, and the world famous Arizona-Sonora Desert Museum was formed. This excellent facility competes with the Grand Canyon as the most visited attraction in Arizona.

In 1961 President John Kennedy added 15,360 acres of federally owned land in Tucson Mountain Park to the Saguaro National Monument, to be administered by the National Park Service. This change of jurisdiction was made specifically to prevent mining claims in the area and to preserve the natural beauty. Because of this move, the Tucson Mountain Park was reduced to 13,628 acres, to which an additional 3,000 acres were added in 1974, as a result of a bond election.

As you will see in the following descriptions, the trails in the Tucson Mountains are not difficult. Several are rated as "easy." A good introduction to this area is to hike the David Yetman Trail, using a two-car shuttle. The Hugh Norris Trail to the summit of Wasson Peak is the most difficult trail, but the one that provides the best views of the Tucson area. A final note: These mountains are ideal for winter hiking and cool early spring and late fall days. By summer, it is way too hot.

Hugh Norris Trail

General Description: *A pleasant ridge ramble past an old mine, to the highest peak in the Tucson Mountains*

Difficulty: *Moderate, some areas of steep switchbacks*

Best Time of Year to Hike: *Winter*

Length: *9.8 miles, round-trip*

Miles to Trailhead from Speedway/Campbell Intersection: *19 miles*

Directions to Trailhead from Speedway/Campbell Intersection: *Go west on Speedway 11.8 miles to the intersection of Kinney Road. (Note: At the intersection of Anklam Road, Speedway becomes Gates Pass Road.) Turn right on Kinney Road, following the signs to Saguaro National Park. The entrance to the park is past the Arizona-Sonora Desert Museum, is signed, and is to the right. Turn into the park and drive past the Red Hills Information Center to Hohokam Road. Turn right. The Hugh Norris trailhead is 0.8 of a mile ahead. There is a small parking area on the right.*

My favorite route to the summit of Wasson Peak is the Hugh Norris Trail. Although longer than other routes, the climb is gradual, and the views from the ridges are spectacular. Wasson Peak offers an unforgettable 360-degree view of the Tucson valley.

This excellent trail is named for Hugh Norris, a Tohono O'odham police chief. The peak it reaches was named for John Wasson, a colorful, often controversial, early editor of the *Tucson Citizen,* who, much to his surprise, was appointed surveyor general of the Arizona Territory in 1870. Although he had absolutely no experience in the field, he retained the position until 1882, when he moved to California.

Signs at the beginning of the Hugh Norris Trail are typical of the trailheads in the Saguaro National Park. Pets are prohibited, as are bicycles, motor vehicles, and weapons. A map depicts the trails of the Park, listing the distances in both miles and kilometers. There is also

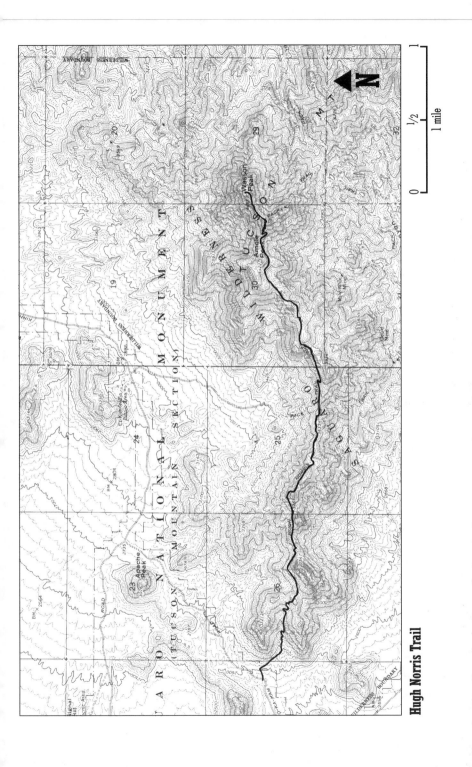

Hugh Norris Trail

0   ½   1

1 mile

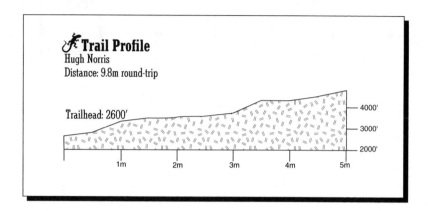

🦎 Trail Profile
Hugh Norris
Distance: 9.8m round-trip

a trail register. It's fun to read the register and note where the hikers came from, especially in winter, when people converge on Tucson from all over the United States and world. These registers serve other purposes. The rangers can judge trail usage, and, in case of the necessity for a search and rescue operation, searchers can tell if the lost hiker did indeed go on this trail. A final sign indicates that the trailhead elevation is 2,600 feet.

The trail climbs gradually at first and then becomes steeper. The only difficulty is stepping over the rocks placed across the trail to prevent erosion. After about a quarter of a mile the trail crosses a deep, sandy drainage, climbs out, and heads up the canyon directly between two ridges. As you gain in elevation, look back at the saguaro forest. There is no place like this in the world. Thousands of giant saguaros spread across the *bajada,* a Spanish term indicating the transition zone between the mountain and the valley. Beyond the saguaros are the farms of Avra Valley. What appears to be a very straight road across the edge of the farm area is actually the canal of the Central Arizona Project (CAP), which delivers water from the Colorado River to Phoenix and Tucson. CAP water use is controversial in Tucson and is not being piped to homes or businesses. As a result of popular vote in 1995, CAP water is currently being used to recharge the aquifer.

As the drainage narrows, the trail steepens and becomes a series of switchbacks that lead to the top of the ridge. To the north, where the walls of the drainage provide protection for the tiny saguaro seeds, there are many young saguaros. This is a pretty, quiet area. The sounds of planes overhead and the occasional pecking of a wood-

Tucson and the Santa Catalinas from Wasson Peak

pecker or chirping of other birds is all you hear. You can easily reach the top of this first ridge in forty-five minutes.

On top of the ridge, the trail turns to the right and is level, then quickly turns left, around the side, and gradually switchbacks to the top of a small saddle. In this saddle there are several side paths that lead to the viewpoints on both sides of the saddle, where there are many boulders that make a good lunch or snack spot.

From this saddle the trail descends briefly, crosses a longer saddle, and begins a long trek along the north side of the ridge. This is a very pleasant portion of the trail. There is some slight elevation gain but nothing serious. The trail is now basically a ridge trail, meandering from one side of the ridge to the other and occasionally going along the top. The views change from one side to the other, first the Catalinas, then Picacho Peak, then the Santa Ritas or Rincons. Below and to the northwest, the Sendero Esperanza Trail winds its way through the basin and up the ridge. Far to the north and high on the ridge, you can see where the Hugh Norris Trail continues its climb to Wasson Peak.

After leveling out on top of the ridge, the trail passes a fenced mine to the right with the warning sign that says, "Peligro Excavacion" or "Danger Excavation." Yet there are signs of where people have crawled under the fence to explore just a little farther, a dangerous practice that has led to the loss of several lives in the Tucson Mountains. A quarter of a mile past the pit and around the east side of the ridge is a signed trail intersection.

This is a good resting spot and meeting place for people who have arranged car swaps to prevent the retracing of steps. For example, one car can be left at the Sendero Esperanza Trailhead, another at Hugh Norris, and still another at King Canyon. All hikers can converge on Wasson Peak and return by a different route. The Hugh Norris Trail continues straight past the intersection and along the ridge for 2.2 miles to the summit of Wasson Peak.

From the intersection, it is a gradual climb along the northwestern side of the ridge. As on the first section of the trail, the rocks placed on the trail for erosion control are the only problem with the trail. After half a mile the trail crosses a short saddle, from which the hiker can see both sides of the mountain. As you look ahead to the peaks, it is difficult to figure out which one is actually Wasson. It is not the one it appears to be, but the peak farthest away and to the left. After the saddle the trail crosses back to the western side of the ridge. At a small sign marking the 4,000-foot elevation level, the trail turns to the right and quickly left across another short saddle, following the east side of the ridge along a smooth, sandy trail.

The trail from this point again meanders from one side of the ridge to the other, interspersed with small saddles. It is smooth and not at all difficult. From this portion of the trail you can see more extensive evidence of the mining that took place in the Tucson Mountains in the early 1900s and again in the 1940s.

Most of the last half-mile of the trail is a series of steep switchbacks. The large rock outcropping directly ahead of the switchbacks is not Wasson Peak, as you will shortly realize, although from the switchbacks it appears to be the high point. Wasson Peak is now visible on the left. At the top of the switchbacks is a signed trail intersection. The King Canyon trailhead is 3.2 miles down the other side of the ridge. The Hugh Norris Trail continues an easy 0.3 of a mile to the summit.

Right before the summit is a trail sign-in box. It is interesting to read the comments of hikers who have reached this vantage point. People from all over the United States have signed the trail registers, with comments like "Better than Mount Rainier!" "A fantastic day," and frequently, just "Wow!" On a clear day, you can see all of Tucson and the surrounding mountains. The comments are understandable.

King Canyon Trail

General Description: *A hike up a canyon past petroglyphs and old mines, to the intersection of the Hugh Norris Trail, near the top of Wasson Peak*

Difficulty: *Moderate, short areas of moderate climbing*

Best Time of Year to Hike: *Winter*

Length: *7 miles, round-trip*

Miles to Trailhead from Speedway/Campbell Intersection: *14.6 miles*

Directions to Trailhead from Speedway/Campbell Intersection: *Go west on Speedway, over Gates Pass to the intersection of Kinney Road. Turn right on Kinney Road, to the Arizona-Sonora Desert Museum. The parking area for the King Canyon Trail is 0.1 of a mile past the entrance to the museum and on the right.*

In 1917 the Copper King Mine was developed in this canyon. Although the mine has been long since abandoned, the trail up the canyon now bears the name of the mine and is known as the King Canyon Trail. In combination with the Hugh Norris Trail, the King Canyon Trail is the shortest route to the summit of Wasson Peak.

Signs at the trailhead warn about the open mine shafts. A sign also notes that one quart of water is the minimum that a hiker should carry to hike this trail. On warm days, one quart is not enough. It is always better to have more water than necessary. The sign also indicates that King Canyon has the only permanent source of water in the Tucson Mountains, but don't count on finding it.

The trail begins as an old jeep road and for the first mile is a wide, rocky walk along the west side of the ridge. Most of the year the canyon drainage is dry, but in times of heavy rain, the rush of water would be an awesome sight. Soon you can see the picnic shelter of the Mam-A-Gah picnic area and the rock building that serves as a rest room below it.

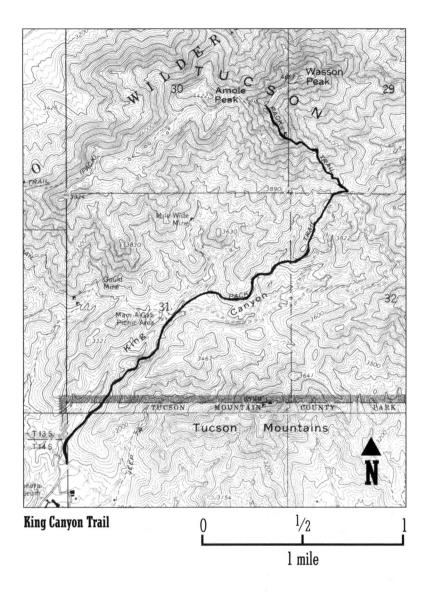

King Canyon Trail

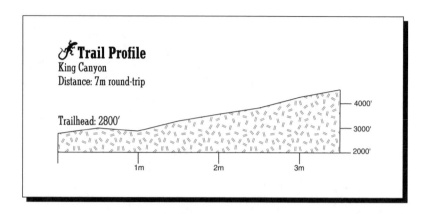

𓃰 Trail Profile
King Canyon
Distance: 7m round-trip

Trailhead: 2800′

4000′

3000′

2000′

1m   2m   3m

As the road approaches the intersection, it drops into and crosses the canyon. Off the trail and to the left, about 1/4 of a mile down the canyon drainage and immediately past a small dam, are many petroglyphs. On both sides of the drainage are many etched drawings that were made by Hohokam Indians, who lived in these mountains from A.D. 900 to 1300. Some of the drawings are intricate, and others look like a child's scribbling. If you are hiking just the King Canyon Trail, you can save this exploration for the return trip, because the wash can be followed almost to the highway, where a path leads up to the parking lot. If you are trading keys with a fellow hiker and will not return by this route, it is worth the short side trip to see the petroglyphs.

As you cross the canyon bottom, a short side trail to the left leads up to the Mam-A-Gah picnic area, where there are six tables and one ramada. This frequently used picnic area is named for the "deer dance" of the Tohono O'odham Indians. The King Canyon Trail turns to the right, past the rest rooms.

The Sendero Esperanza Trailhead is immediately past the rest rooms and to the left. King Canyon Trail is straight ahead and, as the sign indicates, reaches Wasson Peak in 2.6 miles.

Past the intersection, the trail narrows and continues up the canyon. No longer a jeep road, the trail is now very rocky, and sturdy hiking boots are a necessity. In about 200 yards the trail crosses another drainage and then goes along a low ridge between King Canyon and the side drainage for a short distance, before beginning to climb. To the east is an old mine road built when hope was high for the mining potential in these mountains.

Petroglyphs near the King Canyon Trail

The Mile Wide Mining Company owned the claims in this area, and geologist reports were optimistic. Charles F. Willis, geologist and editor of the *Arizona Mining Journal,* said in August 1916, "the Mile Wide Copper Company is destined to become one of the large producers for which the State of Arizona is so well known . . . the property has everything pointing toward success and absolutely none of the signboards of failure." The company named their main mine the Copper King, lowered shafts to a depth of 400 feet, and excavated tunnels. Mining was carried out in 1917 and 1918 and again briefly in 1943, but was never the hoped-for success. The Copper King passed through several owners before being abandoned altogether, achieving a total production of only 1,400 tons. All that remains today are the scars.

The trail continues to climb along the east side of the hill and is easy to follow. In about 1 mile, it reaches the top of the ridge and again becomes an abandoned road. If you are hiking here in early spring, which arrives in late February, this area is usually dotted with wildflowers. If the rains have been sufficient and the winter not too cold, tiny golden poppies peak up through the rocks. Look closely and you will see other varieties. It is one of the mysteries of nature that these flowers can survive the harsh conditions that exist in these mountains.

The road winds around the side of the hill and comes to the intersection of the Sweetwater Trail. Now, for the first time on the King Canyon Trail, you can see the other side of the mountain and the western end of the Santa Catalina Range. It is now only 1.2 miles to Wasson Peak; however, it is a steep 1.2 miles.

From this intersection the trail climbs steeply to the west. The main obstacles on the trail are the large rocks carefully placed to prevent erosion. The peak directly above you is not Wasson. As you climb, the trail becomes a series of switchbacks that climb steadily. There are several fenced mine shafts along this portion of the trail, all with warning signs. As you switchback up the trail, more mines become visible, some in places that look totally inaccessible. You wonder why that particular site was chosen, since the terrain is so rugged and barren.

As the trail reaches the top of the switchbacks, most of the city is visible and Wasson Peak stands out to the north. As the trail levels along the north side of the ridge, you can see the trail intersection sign ahead. Another fenced mine is on the right, with the warning sign in Spanish, "Peligro Excavacion." Past this mine, the trail is level briefly and then climbs in a few switchbacks to the trail intersection. This is the end of the King Canyon Trail. To reach Wasson Peak, follow the Hugh Norris Trail 0.3 of a mile to the summit. The final section is easy and well worth the brief climb required.

Sendero Esperanza Trail

General Description: *A short trail across a ridge, with great views in all directions*

Difficulty: *Moderate, some areas of steep switchbacks*

Best Time of Year to Hike: *Winter*

Length: *3.2 miles, one way*

Miles to Trailhead from Speedway/Campbell Intersection: *22.2 miles*

Directions to Trailhead from Speedway/Campbell Intersection: *Go west on Speedway, over Gates Pass, until you reach the intersection of Kinney Road. Just past the Arizona-Sonora Desert Museum, look for the turn into Saguaro National Park. Drive past the Red Hills Information Center. Turn right on Hohokam Road. Hohokam Road is unpaved and becomes one way after the Hugh Norris trailhead. Turn right on Golden Gate Road, to the parking area for the Sendero Esperanza trailhead. (The ideal way to do this hike is to leave a vehicle at the King Canyon trailhead, 0.1 of a mile on the right, past the Arizona-Sonora Desert Museum, and drive back to pick up the first car or arrange a key swap with friends.)*

Esperanza is Spanish for *hope*, thus, *Sendero Esperanza* is *the trail of hope*. How this name came to be attached to this particular trail is unclear, but one can speculate that, because the trail leads to a large mine, someone once hoped to find riches at the end of the trail!

The Sendero Esperanza Trail climbs the ridge directly to the east of the trailhead and descends on the other side, past the extensive workings of the old Gould Mine, ending at the intersection of the King Canyon Trail, 1 mile north of the Arizona-Sonora Desert Museum. After 1.8 miles, the Sendero Esperanza Trail intersects with the Hugh Norris Trail and makes an excellent route to the top of Wasson Peak.

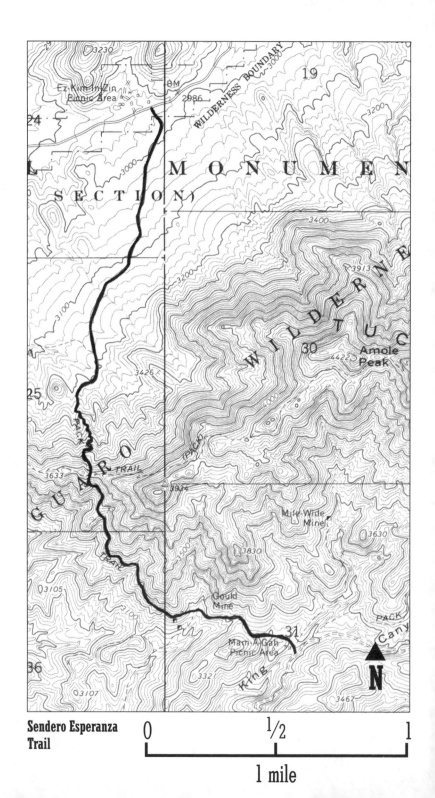

Sendero Esperanza Trail

0   1/2   1

1 mile

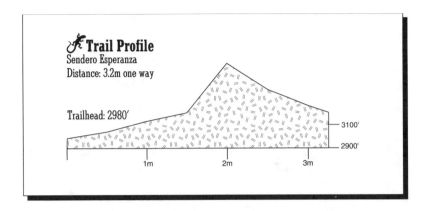

🦎 Trail Profile
Sendero Esperanza
Distance: 3.2m one way

Trailhead: 2980'

— 3100'
— 2900'

1m   2m   3m

From the parking area to Wasson Peak (via the Sendero Esperanza and Hugh Norris Trails), the distance is 4 miles.

Signs at the parking area give a detailed map of the trail system. Pay careful attention to the "Open Mine Shafts—Please Stay on Trail" warning. There are many abandoned mine shafts in the area and lives have been lost by curious explorers who just couldn't resist one more step.

The Sendero Esperanza Trail is flat and sandy for almost the first mile, as it follows a drainage and gains elevation gradually. After the first mile the trail narrows and turns gradually to the right for a short distance, before beginning to climb the switchbacks to the left.

As you look toward the mountain, you can see the ridge that you are about to climb. As you begin to climb the switchbacks, the trail becomes quite rocky in places. The views to the north and northwest are great on a clear day. You can see the mines of the Cyprus Copper Company. The mountain without a top is the limestone quarry for the Portland Cement Company. It is gradually getting smaller, as you will see if you hike this trail again ten years from now. Depending on the time of year, the fields near Marana are squares of green or brown. The triangular outline of Picacho Peak stands out 40 miles north of Tucson. Now a state park, the peak stands in history, a bit erroneously, as the westernmost battle of the Civil War.

As you top the ridge, you come to the well-marked intersection of the Hugh Norris and Sendero Esperanza Trails. From this vantage point, you can see the Red Hills Information Center, the traffic on Kinney Road, and the Santa Rita Mountains to the south. Mount

Powder House—Gould Mine, Sendero Esperanza Trail

Wrightson and Mount Hopkins are the dominant peaks in this range. The Sendero Esperanza Trail drops to the other side of the ridge, past the Mam-A-Gah picnic area, to intersect with the King Canyon Trail.

The trail descends immediately down the west side of the ridge. It is quite rocky and can be treacherous, because it switchbacks and curves downward quickly. This rocky portion is short and after a quarter of a mile, the trail intersects with an old mine road. The Sendero Esperanza Trail goes to the left. The old road is smooth and easy to walk on. It remains level, or a very gradual downhill, for a quarter of a mile or so. There are abandoned mines along the trail. These mines were operated in the days before environmental protection was an issue, so there are many scars.

The views from the road are excellent. Kitt and Baboquivari Peaks stand out in the distance. The hills, made red by iron oxide, to the west are distinct. There are many old weather-beaten saguaros along the road.

Near the bottom of the hill is what remains of the Gould Mine. The *Arizona Daily Star* carried enthusiastic reports of the potential of the mine, stating on May 17, 1905, "the Gould people talk as if they have the biggest bonanza in the territory." By December 21, reports said, "the Gould was working day and night." On July 7, 1907, the *Star* reported "15 wagons carrying ore from the Gould Mine to the Southern Pacific for shipment to El Paso." The Gould Mine worked at a depth of 360 feet and was in production intermittently from 1905 until 1912. Despite the optimism, the total production of the Gould Mine was only 1,500 tons. The owners were forced into bankruptcy in 1915. A fenced shaft, partially covered by boards, a few old beams on the side of the hill, and, 100 yards past the mine, a stone powder house, are all that remains of the Gould Mine today.

Just past the Gould Mine, the road crosses a deep drainage that runs immediately after a rain. On both sides of the drainage is evidence of other mines. Across the drainage the trail climbs gradually. As you round the bend, the shelter and picnic tables of the Mam-A-Gah picnic area are visible. This is a popular destination for hikers entering from the King Canyon trailhead. As the trail crosses a small drainage, you will notice an unmarked path to the right that leads to the picnic area. The trail continues straight ahead, and in about 200 yards you will come to the official signed path that leads up to the picnic tables. The Sendero Esperanza Trail ends 200 yards past this sign.

A sign indicates that the Arizona-Sonora Desert Museum is 1 mile ahead. The King Canyon trailhead is 0.9 of a mile along the road across the wash. There are rest rooms to the right. If you are doing a key swap or have a vehicle at the King Canyon trailhead, continue on the King Canyon Trail to the parking area; otherwise return to the Sendero Esperanza trailhead by retracing your steps.

Sweetwater Trail

General Description: *An enjoyable climb through one of the most varied stands of saguaro in the Tucson Mountains*

Difficulty: *Moderate*

Best Time of Year to Hike: *Spring, Fall, Winter*

Length: *6.4 miles, round-trip*

Miles to Trailhead from Speedway/Campbell Intersection: *15 miles*

Directions to Trailhead from Speedway/Campbell Intersection: *Drive north on Campbell Avenue to Fort Lowell Road. Turn left on Fort Lowell Road to Stone Avenue. Turn right on Stone Avenue to Wetmore Road. Turn left on Wetmore Road. Continue on Wetmore to Romero Road. Turn right on Romero. Romero becomes Ruthrauff at the curve, which becomes El Camino del Cerro after passing under Interstate 10. Continue on El Camino del Cerro until it dead-ends at the trailhead. A paved trailhead parking area has room for fifteen cars and two horsetrailers.*

Find a guide to plants of the Sonoran Desert and head for the Sweetwater Trail. It's a virtual botanical classroom, with emphasis on saguaro in various stages of growth.

This trail was for a long time inaccessible because it required crossing private land to reach the trailhead. A new trailhead parking area and connecting link, constructed as a joint effort between Pima County and the Saguaro National Park, now makes the Sweetwater Trail accessible to hikers and horseback riders. A sign at the trailhead indicates that the Sweetwater Trail meets the King Canyon Trail in 3.2 miles. From this intersection, it is only 1.2 miles to Wasson Peak, the high point of the Tucson Mountains.

The trail begins as a level walk along a low ridge. In about 0.2 mile a sign indicates that the Sweetwater Trail turns left and drops into a deep wash. You'll see the first of several large pack rat nests in this

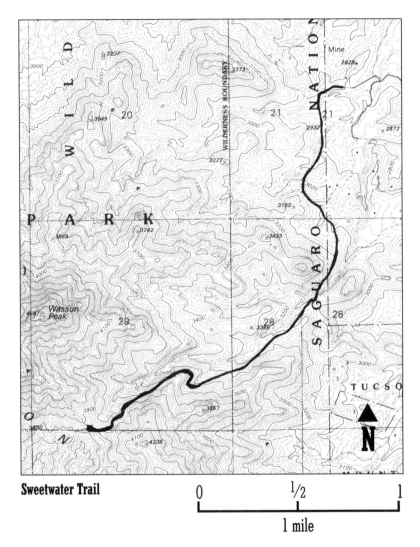

Sweetwater Trail

0   ½   1

1 mile

section. In his excellent treatise on the Sonoran Desert, *House in the Sun,* George Olin says that pack rats are often called "trade" rats because while they are in the process of carrying a prized item to their nest, they may find something they like better and trade the original item for the newer prize, often leaving a trail of watches, pocket knives, and other treasures in the vicinity of their nests. Pack rat nests

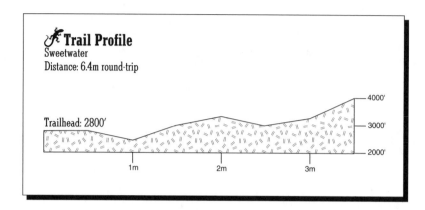

are built of wood, sticks, and branches, and covered with the spines of a teddy bear cholla to protect them from predators. As you will note along this trail, their nests can be quite substantial.

After crossing the wash, the trail climbs the ridge and provides excellent views of the city to the east and Wasson Peak to the west. It is easy to follow and in one section it includes a series of switchbacks and steps. Side trails have been disguised by extensive plantings of prickly pear and cholla.

A little over half way into the hike, the new section of the trail joins the original trail and becomes more difficult to hike. The older trail is narrow and rocky in comparison with the wider and smoother new section. Still, it is relatively easy and, as the trail climbs toward the saddle, provides ever more dramatic views of the Tucson valley to the east and Wasson Peak to the northwest.

Of particular interest is the large number of saguaro in all stages of growth. The saguaro thrives on southern exposures and near the washes. Younger plants from one to three feet tall are abundant, as are several giants, which must be over one hundred years old.

The Sweetwater Trail ends in a small saddle. From here it is possible to continue on to Wasson Peak via the King Canyon and Hugh Norris Trails, or to go down the mountain on the King Canyon Trail to the parking area across the road from the Arizona-Sonora Desert Museum. The trail network in the Saguaro National Park provides numerous possibilities for key exchanges. Wasson Peak can be reached from the King Canyon, Hugh Norris, Sendero Esperanza, and Sweetwater trailheads.

A newly constructed section of the Sweetwater Trail

David Yetman Trail

General Description: *An easy walk through typical vegetation of the Sonoran Desert*

Difficulty: *Moderate, few areas with slight elevation gain*

Best Time of Year to Hike: *Winter*

Length: *5.4 miles, with two vehicles*

Miles to Trailhead from Speedway/Campbell Intersection: *10.1 miles to parking area on west side of Gates Pass*

Directions to Trailhead from Speedway/Campbell Intersection: *The Yetman Trail has two trailheads. It is possible to leave cars at each trailhead and work out combinations that enable you not to have to retrace steps. A good combination that makes most of the hike downhill is to leave a vehicle at the Camino de Oeste trailhead and continue to the Gates Pass trailhead. To do this from the Speedway/Campbell intersection, go west on Speedway. Shortly after passing the West Anklam Road/Speedway intersection, turn left on Camino de Oeste. Drive carefully up the unpaved road, until it dead-ends with a parking area on the right, and leave a car. Continue on Speedway, which is now called Gates Pass Road, across Gates Pass and down the west side of the mountain, to a large parking area on the left, almost at the bottom of the mountain. This is the starting point for the David Yetman and Golden Gate Trails.*

D avid Yetman was a member of the Pima County Board of Supervisors from 1977 to 1988. Sometimes controversial, Yetman became known for his fervent defense of the environment. The Yetman Trail, which crosses a lovely area in the Tucson Mountains, was named in his honor when he retired from the board of supervisors.

The David Yetman Trail is marked by a sign on the left. The trail begins on an old mine, or jeep, road. It goes between two peaks, to the right of a large drainage, and is at first a gradual incline before lev-

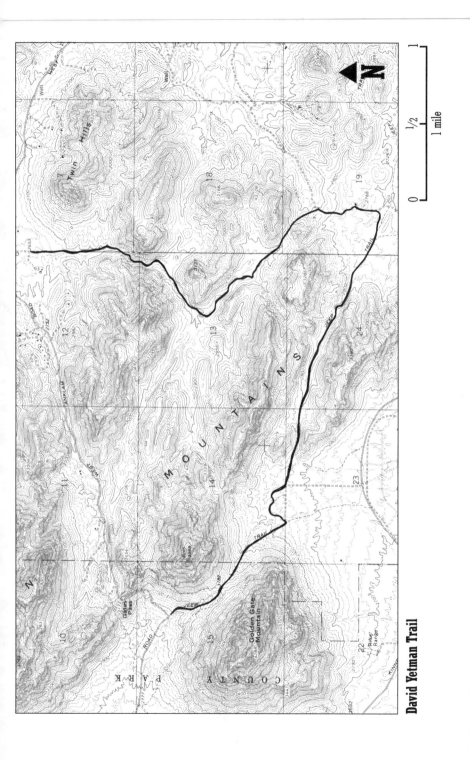

David Yetman Trail

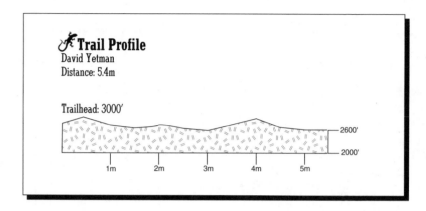

🦎 **Trail Profile**
David Yetman
Distance: 5.4m

Trailhead: 3000'

2600'
2000'

1m 2m 3m 4m 5m

eling off. After about 3/4 of a mile, signs indicate the intersection of three trails—the Golden Gate Trail to the right, the Gates Pass Trail to the left, and the David Yetman Trail straight ahead.

The Yetman Trail goes through the pass and continues downhill. This is an easy trail and is perfect for people who want to become better acquainted with the Sonoran Desert, without too much elevation gain. This portion goes through lots of teddy bear cholla and is very smooth. In about 0.5 of a mile a sign indicates that the Yetman Trail bears to the left. This portion of the trail is well marked, as it meanders in and out of small drainages. The trail is a favorite of mountain bikers, and often side trails have been created to climb small hills. Watch carefully for the correct route.

After approximately 0.8 of a mile, a sign indicates that the Yetman Trail bears to the left. Here the trail crosses several washes, before climbing briefly, albeit steeply, to the side of a ridge. Notice that the side of the hill to the left of the wash protects an excellent stand of saguaros. The trail continues along the side of the hill for a short distance before descending into a creek bed. For nearly a mile the trail follows the usually dry creek bed, crossing occasionally from one side to the other.

The trail leaves the creek and is now in the open. It is wide and sandy and, in fact, is almost a road. Signs and sounds of civilization begin to appear—a telephone line and the sound of automobiles. A sign indicates the direction of the David Yetman and Starr Pass Trails. Continue to the left on the David Yetman Trail.

The Yetman Trail goes past the sign, to the left, along an old jeep

Bowen House on the David Yetman Trail

road. The road drops into a wash and begins a gradual climb uphill. A trail sign indicates that the Yetman trailhead is 1.6 miles to the left.

The trail now becomes narrow and soon parallels the fenced boundary of Tucson Mountain Park. The structure to the right and across the drainage is a storage facility for the Central Arizona Project. Also visible from this section of the trail are the downtown Tucson area and the Catalina Mountains. There is an unusual number of young saguaros along the east side of the ridge, probably one hundred or more in the fifteen- to twenty-five-year-old range. The trail is narrow, has lots of loose rocks, and climbs rather steeply to the top of the ridge, where the other side of the mountain, including Gates Pass, is visible.

Two trails leave the ridge. Take the one headed straight downhill. This is a very pleasant part of the trail. It goes gently downhill through a level valley. There is no sign of civilization here, and it is very peaceful. In early spring there is a scattering of golden Mexican poppies and other wildflowers in this valley. Small "Trail" signs indicate the correct route, which, at this point, drops into a creek bed, whose sandy bottom makes for more difficult walking.

A short way down the wash, a path leads to the left out of the wash to a stone house. The house has no roof, and the structure shows signs of fire damage, still the sturdy walls remain. The house was built in the early 1930s by Sherry Bowen, a typesetter and, later, city editor for the *Arizona Daily Star.* Sherry brought his wife, Ruby, to Tucson from Rockford, Illinois, in the late 1920s, hoping that the climate would help her serious heart condition. They first lived in Tucson, but soon homesteaded in the Tucson Mountains, eventually owning 2,000 acres. They moved to the homestead in 1931, living in a cabin while the house was being built.

Ruby Bowen kept a diary of her first year in the Tucson Mountains. She talks of the wild mountain sheep that came to the base of the cliffs to graze nearly every evening and then majestically climbed the steep canyon walls, to return to a cave that was their home. A mountain lion would pace about when Ruby was cooking meat and one time attempted to get in the window. Javelina, deer, and even a herd of wild horses came into their canyon.

The recuperative powers of the desert worked. The Bowens' daughter was born in 1943. They left Tucson in 1944 for New York City, where Sherry Bowen worked for the Associated Press. The valley and their homestead became part of Tucson Mountain Park in 1983.

The trail passes to the left of the house, crosses the creek, and again follows the creek bed, now a wide, sandy one. The trail follows the wide creek bed to the trailhead. On the left side of the creek there are hundreds of healthy saguaros. Unfortunately, many of the saguaros have been vandalized; cut at about the 4-foot level. Many survived this vicious attack and now have several arms rising above the cuts. In early spring the creek bed is covered with an assortment of wildflowers. The trailhead marks the boundary of the Tucson Mountain Park. To reach your car, you'll need to walk a little farther along on an unpaved road, through privately owned land, until you come to the Camino de Oeste parking lot.

Golden Gate Loop Trail

General Description: *An easy hike around the mountain that is used as the backdrop in many western movies*

Difficulty: *Easy, few areas with moderate elevation gain*

Best Time of Year to Hike: *Winter, late fall, early spring*

Length: *6.6 miles for the loop*

Miles to Trailhead from Speedway/Campbell Intersection: *10.1 miles*

Directions to Trailhead from Speedway/Campbell Intersection: *Go west on Speedway, over Gates Pass to the parking area on the left, near the bottom of the mountain. (Past Anklam Road, Speedway becomes Gates Pass Road.) This is the trailhead for the David Yetman Trail. The Golden Gate trailhead is 0.5 of a mile along the Yetman Trail.*

The Golden Gate Trail circles Golden Gate Mountain. Legend has it that the mountain was so named because early prospectors thought Gates Pass and the mountain constituted the gate to the gold in the Tucson Mountains.

Whatever the reason for the mountain's name, the Golden Gate is a beautiful trail that can be hiked in combination with other trails, to form a loop to return to the parking lot. As is true of most of the trails in the Tucson Mountains, the Golden Gate Trail is basically a desert ramble. At first the desert appears barren, but an experienced hiker learns to look for the small things—the colorful lizard scurrying out of his way, the magenta bloom of a hedgehog cactus in spring, the teddy bear cholla glistening in the sun. The desert is s special place—one that you will learn to appreciate as you hike the trails.

From the parking area, proceed up the David Yetman Trail for about 0.5 of a mile to a signed intersection. The Golden Gate Trail is to the right. It is well constructed and easy to follow. At first the trail is narrow and lined with rocks. In about 100 yards the trail drops into and

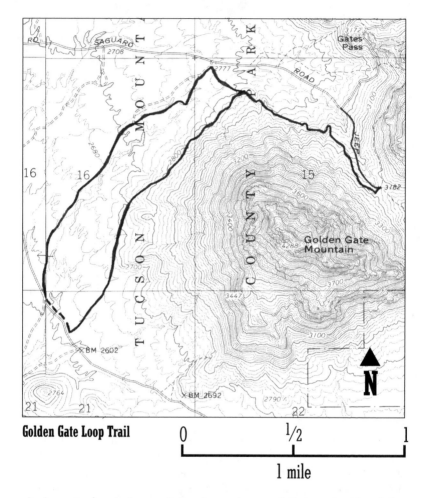

Golden Gate Loop Trail

0   1/2   1

1 mile

climbs out of a drainage. It heads west around the north side of the mountain, dropping in and out of drainages. In these drainages the vegetation is thicker, and the area is quite pretty. After about 0.5 of a mile the trail goes downhill more steeply. It is rocky, and sturdy hiking boots are a must. One particular drainage is full of teddy bear cholla and, if the light is right, the shiny needles make for striking pictures. Several of the cholla contain the intricate cone-shaped nests made by the cactus wren. These nests are works of art, fitting securely in the spiny cholla. There are very few saguaro along this first part of the trail.

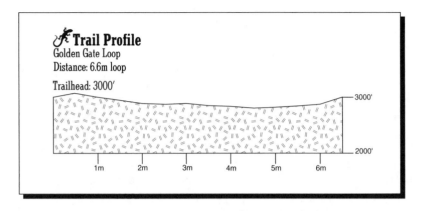

𓆲 Trail Profile
Golden Gate Loop
Distance: 6.6m loop

Trailhead: 3000'

The trail works its way in and out of drainages, turning first north, then south, then west again, remaining along the north side of Golden Gate Mountain. There are nice views to the west. Miles of saguaro spread out across the basin. Far in the distance you can see the buildings of the Arizona-Sonora Desert Museum. The trail alternates from being smooth to going through sections of baseball-sized rocks, all the while dropping in and out of small drainages. Spring is the ideal time to hike in this area, when magenta hedgehogs, orange ocotillo, yellow prickly pear, and the white saguaro blossoms make the desert a colorful place.

Many large boulders have tumbled down from Golden Gate Mountain. The terrain of the Tucson Mountains is what geologists call *chaos,* a most descriptive term.

After about 3/4 of a mile the trail comes around the bend in the mountain, and you can see Old Tucson Studios for the first time. Built in 1939 by Columbia Pictures for the filming of the first outdoor color western, *Arizona,* the set has been home to many Westerns over the years, such as *Gunfight at the O.K. Corral, Rio Bravo, Cimarron,* and *Three Amigos.* In later years the television series *Gunsmoke, High Chaparral,* and *Bonanza* were filmed in the area. More recently, *Young Riders* brought action to Old Tucson. In a spectacular fire, most of Old Tucson burned in the summer of 1995, but it has since been restored.

Soon the trail goes down the side of the mountain and heads west along the flat basins. As you pass a huge pile of boulders on the left, the trail divides and becomes, for the first time, confusing. Turn left toward the rocks, but do not continue past the rocks. Instead, turn right. A line of rocks marks the trail that you should use. Other trails lead to the boulders and beyond, but the Golden Gate Trail is clearly marked and goes to the west, almost immediately crossing a small drainage.

For most of this part of the trail you can see Old Tucson. The trail is now level and makes for easy, pleasant walking. To the left are excellent views of Golden Gate Mountain. After 1/4 of a mile you come to an intersection. Again, you should continue straight ahead along the trail that is marked by a line of rocks. As you circle Golden Gate Mountain, you go in and out of several small drainages. Again, there are patches of cholla. This is a popular route for horseback riders and occasionally a mountain biker. It is a peaceful section, and, although you are clearly near civilization and tour buses, it seems that you are alone in the desert.

The trail continues southwest away from Old Tucson, and soon you can no longer see the movie set. Most of the hikes in the Tucson Mountains lead to the tops of mountains. It is a good change to be down in the basin looking up. Baboquivari and Kitt Peaks are visible. For a short period you can see Mount Wrightson, to the south. As the trail nears the road, it becomes very flat and smooth. This trail ends at Kinney Road, which in the tourist season can be very busy.

Here you have two alternatives. You can retrace your steps or walk a short distance on the right side of Kinney Road, to the next parking area, and take the trail past Old Tucson to return to the Golden Gate Trail. If you choose this option, turn right and walk along the road 0.4 of a mile to the first parking area on your right. The trail begins between the yellow barriers. This is an easy, pleasant walk along an old road, with Old Tucson on the left and Golden Gate Mountain on the right. After about 3/4 of a mile, the road narrows into a trail, again lined with rocks. Notice the number of "nurse trees" sheltering small saguaros.

As the trail circles away from Golden Gate Mountain and heads toward Gates Pass Road (Saguaro Road on map), you soon join an old road that goes toward Gates Pass Road. Follow this road across a wide drainage, to a large parking area beside Gates Pass Road. A well-defined trail leaves this parking area and heads toward Golden Gate Mountain. It is a wide path that leads toward the large pile of boulders where you began the loop part of this hike. At the intersection just

Golden Gate Mountain—The background for many Western movies

before the boulders, go straight even though it appears that you should turn left. It is 0.5 of a mile back to the parking lot. As you near the parking area, you can see your car, and it is tempting to bush-whack down into the ravine and scramble up the side to the car. Hav-ing tried this, I can advise that it is much easier to follow the trail to the Yetman Trail intersection and return to the parking lot via the wide road.

Kinney Road Access Trail

General Description: *An easy connecting trail to use for a loop hike with the David Yetman Trail*

Difficulty: *Easy*

Best Time of Year to Hike: *Winter*

Length: *2.8 miles, round-trip*

Miles to Trailhead from Speedway/Campbell Intersection: *11.9 miles*

Directions to Trailhead from Speedway/Campbell Intersection: *To reach the Kinney Road Access trailhead, go west on Speedway to Interstate 10. Go east on I-10 2.7 miles to the I-19 exit. Exit on I-19 and go 1.3 miles to the Ajo Way exit. Follow Ajo Way 5.2 miles to Kinney Road. Turn right on Kinney Road and go 2 miles to Tucson Estates Parkway. This road is easy to miss. It is 0.3 of a mile past the Western Way intersection. Turn right on Tucson Estates Parkway. The trailhead is on an unpaved road to the left and is visible right before you reach the gate of The Foothills housing development. A large sign says, "Tucson Mountain Park Main Entrance."*

This popular trail connects with the David Yetman Trail and is frequently used by the residents of Tucson Mountain Estates and The Foothills. A number of combinations can be worked out involving the David Yetman, Starr Pass, and Kinney Road Access Trails.

In the parking area a sign says, "Trail Ahead." Turn right immediately. The trail drops steeply into a drainage before heading across the flat desert. It then veers right again, heading directly toward Golden Gate Mountain. The trail rambles across small drainages, but is never difficult. On this lower portion of the trail, you can sometimes

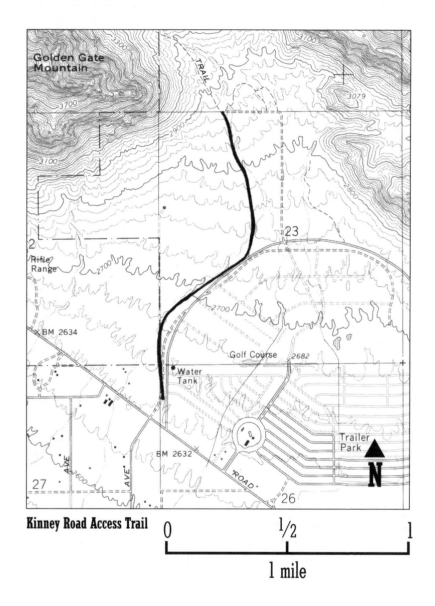

Kinney Road Access Trail

0   1/2   1

1 mile

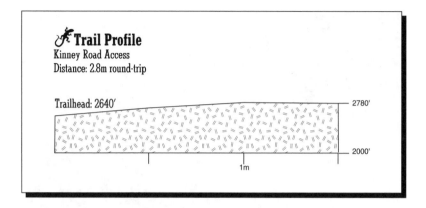

❧ **Trail Profile**
Kinney Road Access
Distance: 2.8m round-trip

Trailhead: 2640'   — 2780'

                                                                     — 2000'

1m

hear shots from the Tucson Mountain Park Rifle Range. After about 1/2 of a mile, you can see two large tanks, which you later learn are water storage tanks and part of the City of Tucson water system.

Saguaros are scarce in this area, although there are a few giants and a number of small ones growing in the shelter of the palo verde trees. Unfortunately, this is not a quiet desert ramble. In addition to the sounds of the rifle range and the automobiles on Kinney Road, there are sounds of jets approaching to land at Tucson International Airport and Davis Monthan Air Force Base. The trail soon intersects with an old road and follows the road to the right. The road goes to the water facility. As you near the tanks, another road leads straight to the parking area for the trailhead, and you can see your car. This is a private road, however, and, when you return to your car, you should use the trail.

Just before the water tanks, the trail turns to the right. It is possible to continue past the water tanks to the left and end up at the base of the cliffs. This is a difficult trail, but its elevation gain provides good views of the area. The correct trail is wide, smooth, and sandy. It meanders across the desert, crossing small drainages. It is a very pleasant stroll. After 0.2 of a mile the trail forks to the right, but you should continue straight ahead. The general direction of the trail is to the north, toward the pass between the mountains. The trail is generally easy to follow. At one point there is a definite fork, and, because it is unsigned, it is confusing. Either fork is all right to follow, because the two trails converge after a short distance. Past this fork, the trail crosses a deeper drainage that could have water after a rain. After 1 mile the

Kinney Road Access Trail

trail comes to an intersection with an old road. Mountain bikers have permission to use the trails of the Tucson Mountains, and this trail is very popular. Two large cairns (piles of rocks) mark this spot. Turn to the left, toward the mountains. After a short distance and a gradual elevation gain, you come to a triangular fork in the road. A sign indicates that this is the David Yetman Trail. From here the Kinney Road hiker can go right to the Camino de Oeste trailhead or left to the Gates Pass trailhead. It is fun to arrange a three-car hike, trade car keys along the trail, and meet at a restaurant for lunch.

Starr Pass Trail

General Description: *A short trail through a spectacular low mountain pass that serves as a connecting trail with other trails in the Tucson Mountains*

Difficulty: *Easy*

Best Time of Year to Hike: *Winter*

Length: *2.2 miles, round-trip*

Miles to Trailhead from Speedway/Campbell Intersection: *12.1 miles*

Directions to Trailhead from Speedway/Campbell Intersection: *To reach the Starr Pass trailhead, go west on Speedway to Interstate 10. Go east on I-10 2.7 miles to the I-19 exit. Exit on I-19 and go 1.3 miles to the Ajo Way exit. Follow Ajo Way 5.2 miles to Kinney Road. Turn right on Kinney Road, go 0.8 of a mile to Sarasota Boulevard. Turn right on Sarasota and follow the road past the trailer park until it dead-ends. There are two sections of unpaved road. Turn right on the one closest to the fence. The Starr Pass trailhead is 0.1 of a mile on the left, between two fence posts.*

The Starr Pass Trail is only 1.1 miles from the intersection of the David Yetman Trail. I include it in the trail descriptions because it serves as the connecting point for several trails in the Tucson Mountains. For example, you can park one vehicle at the David Yetman-Gates Pass trailhead and another at Starr Pass trailhead, trade car keys, and avoid retracing your path. There are a number of combinations that can be worked out.

Aside from its possibilities as a loop trail, Starr Pass goes through some very unusual terrain, through a low pass with Cat Mountain on the right and an unnamed peak on the left.

Originally built in January 1884 by Richard A. Starr, the trail was a quick route from downtown Tucson to the booming mine town of Quijotoa, 70 miles southwest of Tucson. It was intended as a toll road,

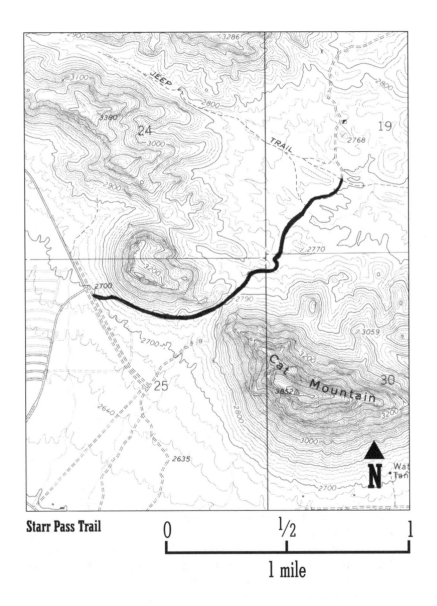

Starr Pass Trail

0   1/2   1

1 mile

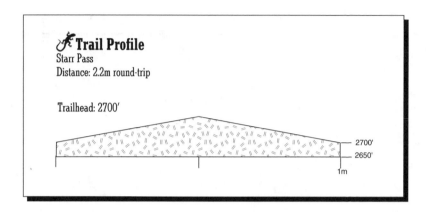

🦎 **Trail Profile**
Starr Pass
Distance: 2.2m round-trip

Trailhead: 2700'

2700'
2650'
1m

but it is doubtful that this was realized, because the mines were played out by 1885. Also in January 1884 the Arizona Telegraph Company was incorporated and planned to connect Tucson and Quijotoa by telegraph. The contract was awarded to R. A. Starr and J. A. Browder, who completed the line in April 1884. Today most of the original Starr Pass Road is part of Tucson Mountain Park.

The area is still a significant part of the Tucson scene. An 8,340-foot tunnel bores its way to the right of the pass, through Cat Mountain, to deliver water from the Central Arizona Project treatment facility to the City of Tucson storage facility near 22nd Street. You can see this facility from the David Yetman Trail as it exits on Camino de Oeste. You may wonder why the tunnel was built when the logical plan would have been to build the storage facility near the treatment plant. According to Al Stites, chief inspector for the tunnel, it cost less to build the tunnel than to purchase property and utility easements. Even at that, the total cost of the tunnel was $12 million.

As is true with most of the trails in this section of the Tucson Mountains, Starr Pass Trail is like a maze. Side trails go off in every direction, and it is sometimes hard to know for sure which route you should take. The trail goes between the opening in the fence, between two posts, and gradually climbs to the right, before bearing to the left and through the pass. The trail is sandy and is easy to walk on at first, but soon goes in and out of several fairly deep drainages.

The main trail enters a small drainage and stays in it for 0.2 of a mile through huge boulders. Many saguaros cling to the sides of the cliff. You pass through the remains of a steel gate, and right past this

Starr Pass Trail

gate, the trail reaches the top of the rise, and you can see the Catalinas to the north. Continue straight ahead, ignoring any side trails for awhile. The trail goes gradually downhill, and this is a pleasant section.

As the trail continues downhill, it briefly enters a section that is rocky and hard to walk on. Right past this section, you come to a trail intersection. Turn to the left. In a short distance there is another fork. This time, do not turn to the left but continue straight ahead. Soon there is another fork. This time keep to the right. Very quickly you come to a signed intersection. This is a major intersection and the place where you can meet other hikers for key exchanges. These trails have become very popular with mountain bikers.

Brown Mountain Trail

General Description: *A ridge hike with spectacular views of the Tucson valley*

Difficulty: *Moderate, few areas of steep climbing*

Best Time of Year to Hike: *Winter, early spring, late fall*

Length: *4.8 miles, round-trip*

Miles to Trailhead from Speedway/Campbell Intersection: *13.5 miles*

Directions to Trailhead from Speedway/Campbell Intersection: *Go west on Speedway, through Gates Pass to the intersection of Kinney Road. (Speedway becomes Gates Pass Road at Anklam Road.) Turn right on Kinney Road to Gilbert Ray Campground entrance (on Mc-Cain Loop Road) and turn left for 0.4 of a mile. The parking area for the trailhead is on the right and is signed. (The ideal way to hike this ridge is to leave a vehicle at the Juan Santa Cruz picnic area 0.2 of a mile beyond the pull-in for the Gilbert Ray Campground, on the left, before the Arizona-Sonora Desert Museum.)*

The Brown Mountain Trail is an unusual trek along a ridge in the heart of the Tucson Mountains. The ridge was named for Cornelius B. Brown, Pima County agricultural agent from 1920 to 1945, who was instrumental in the creation of Tucson Mountain Park in 1929. Brown is remembered as the "Father of Tucson Mountain Park."

The trail leaves from the southwest side of the small parking area and crosses the desert to a deep wash. For much of this hike you will be treated to a saguaro education. Saguaros in all stages of life—from a few inches to over 20 feet tall to ribbed skeletons outlined against the sky are along the trail. Across the wash, the Cougar Trail cuts off to the right. The Brown Mountain Trail continues across a smaller wash and after a rocky 1/4 of a mile, switchbacks up the mountain.

A short elevation gain brings you to the top of the first peak. Look back for sweeping views to the east. Closest to you is Gilbert

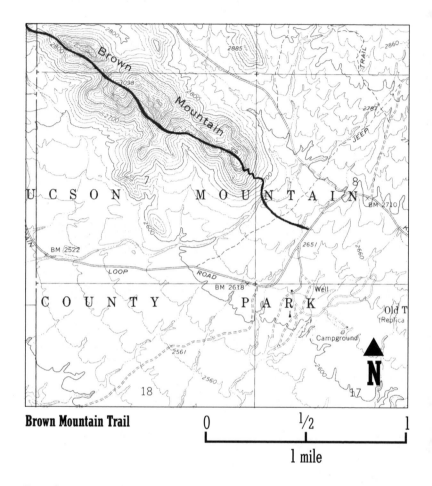

Brown Mountain Trail

0   ¹/₂   1

1 mile

Ray Campground. In winter there are at least a hundred campers in every conceivable type of camping rig, enjoying a respite from northern winters. Old Tucson Studios, a movie set and tourist attraction, is at the base of Golden Gate Mountain. It is the backdrop for many Westerns. This studio was nearly destroyed in a fire in the summer of 1995 but has now been restored.

To the northeast of Old Tucson Studios, Gates Pass winds its way down between the mountains. To the left of Gates Pass and high on the ridge are two houses that look like dollhouses from your vantage point. These homes were the scene of an environmental controversy

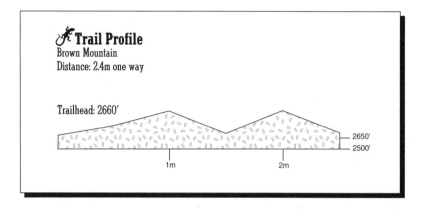

🦎 Trail Profile
Brown Mountain
Distance: 2.4m one way

Trailhead: 2660'

2650'
2500'

1m   2m

in the late 1970s. The homes were built by partners in a construction firm, who were accused of flagrantly violating the community's wishes, by bulldozing a road to the homesite just before the Pima County Board of Supervisors passed an ordinance preventing building on steep slopes and ridges. In 1977 vandals hot-wired a bulldozer and knocked down the walls of the houses, then under construction. The following year, both houses were damaged by fires of suspicious origin.

The controversy resurfaced late in 1986, when the owner of one of the homes requested permission to double the size of his house as well as add a guest house and heliport. After much debate, the Pima County Board of Supervisors approved the expansion of the house but denied permission for the guest house and heliport. The owner agreed to stabilize the road and add vegetation to help conceal the road leading to the houses.

From this point the trail crosses the ridge, going up and down and occasionally along the side of the ridge. The views are always excellent. Several great lookout spots provide views of the western valley, where Baboquivari and Kitt Peaks are the dominant landmarks. Closer in is the Arizona-Sonora Desert Museum, and at the base of the ridge is the Juan Santa Cruz picnic area, where, hopefully, you have a vehicle waiting. To the southwest, you can trace the canal of the Central Arizona Project. (As of this printing the picnic area was closed for renovation. You can park at the entrance gate and walk down to the road.)

Along the ridge you will notice an abundance of small saguaros. From one spot I could count twenty small saguaros, not more than 2 feet tall. This is very unusual, because the area is not a protected one,

Hiker checking saguaro cactus skeleton on Brown Mountain Trail

normally thought capable of supporting such a heavy growth of young cacti. The trail is lined with boulders, and walking through this area is like walking through a well-manicured English garden.

As you come to the end of the ridge, the trail switchbacks sharply down to the Juan Santa Cruz picnic area, where, if you have a vehicle waiting, you hop in and drive back to the trailhead. If not, it's back up the ridge and back to the parking area near the Gilbert Ray Campground. It is, of course, possible to walk back along Kinney Road, but that is a dangerous route, not nearly as pleasant as walking back along the Brown Mountain ridge.

Gilbert Ray Campground Loop Trail

General Description: *A basically flat trail that has many small saguaros thriving under the protection of palo verde trees*

Difficulty: *Easy*

Best Time of Year to Hike: *Winter, early spring, late fall*

Length: *5.3 miles, loop*

Miles to Trailhead from Speedway/Campbell Intersection: *12.5 miles*

Directions to Trailhead from Speedway/Campbell Intersection: *Go west on Speedway, over Gates Pass, to the intersection of Kinney Road. Turn right on Kinney Road and drive for 0.7 of a mile to the Gilbert Ray Campground, which is on the left. Park at the registration building. If anyone is in the office, notify them that you are hiking; otherwise leave a note on the dash of your car. The trail begins on the "A" Loop between camping spaces 52 and 53. A sign indicates "Trail."*

G ilbert Ray was the first director of the Tucson Parks and Recreation Department. From March 1947 until his retirement in December 1972, he oversaw the development of the Tucson parks system. Gilbert Ray Campground Loop Trail circles the campground named in his honor and is perfect for someone who wants to see what it is like out in the desert but is not interested in a strenuous hike. It wanders about with a very minimum of elevation loss and gain—in fact the only variation in the trail is in and out of washes.

The first segment of the trail is for campers who want to walk over to Old Tucson Studios. After about 200 yards, you come to a small wash; a few yards later the trail crosses a deep wash.

Across the wash, the trail is an old road that quickly comes to an intersection with another road. Across the paved road is Old Tucson Studios. Go right on the dirt road and follow the route of the utility

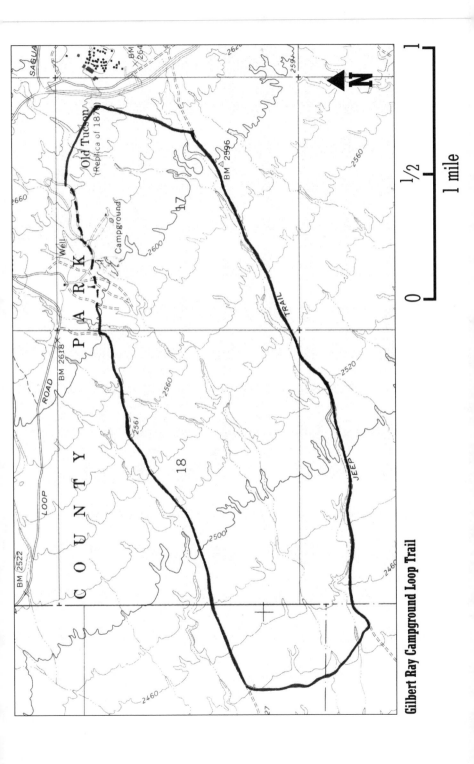

Gilbert Ray Campground Loop Trail

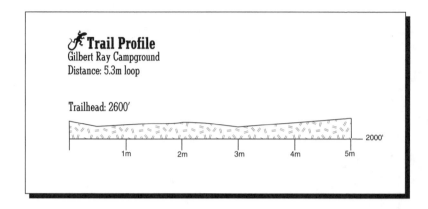

✖Trail Profile
Gilbert Ray Campground
Distance: 5.3m loop

Trailhead: 2600'

line across the desert. The trail is now heading southwest and is basically a utility access road at this point. Probably because it is for the most part a flat trail and easy to access, the Gilbert Ray Campground Loop Trail is popular with horseback riders and mountain bikers, both permitted on the trails of Tucson Mountain Park.

There are mostly old saguaros along the first part of the route. Vegetation increases in drainages, where mesquite and palo verde thrive. Creosote grows in abundance, as do prickly pear, cholla, and barrel cacti. If you are on the trail in the early morning or late afternoon, you may see some javelina or mule deer. Note the pads of the prickly pear that have been eaten by these two desert creatures. The javelina's bite leaves the pads shredded, whereas the mule deer bites off neat chunks.

Along one particularly large drainage, water has cut deep banks. Although the heat would be uncomfortable, it would be interesting to hike this trail after a summer storm, to observe the water swirling through the washes. As the trail progresses it gets farther away from civilization, and, for a short time, the only signs of humans are the utility poles.

After about 2 miles, notice an unusual saguaro on the right, across the wash. Several small arms near its top make it appear fan-shaped. Less than 0.2 of a mile past this saguaro, you spot a mobile home, a stable, and some horses off to the left. When you see the mobile home, begin looking carefully for a turnoff to the right, which is usually marked by several cairns. The correct route is clearly visible. The path, now no longer a road but a narrow trail, turns immediately

A "nurse" tree shelters twelve saguaros on the Gilbert Ray Campground Loop Trail

to the right and crosses a wash. If you made the correct turn, you should be going away from the utility poles and the trailer.

The interesting part of this section of the trail is the number of small saguaros thriving under the palo verde trees. The palo verde trees "nurse" or shelter the saguaros until they are strong enough to thrive on their own. One palo verde tree shelters twelve small saguaros (see photo) with a large packrat nest in the midst of the collection. Packrats are amazing collectors, and it was tempting to break open the mound to see what the little creature had hoarded. Pack rats cover their nests with the spines of teddy bear cholla to protect them from predators.

Unfortunately, pack rats eat saguaro, beginning at the base of larger ones and eating in a spiral, or consuming entire smaller plants. When I last hiked this section, this particular tree protected thirteen saguaros, but now the skeleton of a small one lies on the ground. Pack rats are the main enemies of small saguaros, and, if this pack rat and its offspring continue to live in the shade of this palo verde tree, it is likely that they will destroy the twelve remaining saguaros.

After 1/2 of a mile the trail intersects with an unpaved road. Turn right on the road to return to the campground. The road is a rarely used utility access road. This is a very pleasant walk, mostly flat. There is only one portion where it dips in and out of a small drainage. There are still many palo verde trees with tiny saguaros underneath. This area must be very beautiful in early May when the palo verde trees are covered with tiny yellow blossoms.

As the road curves to the left, or north, you can see the Gilbert Ray Campground, and you know that you should be heading off to the right. Keep looking carefully for a side road that leads to the campground. There is usually a cairn as a marker. Take this road to the right. It drops almost immediately into a deep ravine. There are several underground-cable warning posts. As you come out of the ravine you can see picnic shelters and a paved road.

You are back at the Gilbert Ray Campground and picnic area. Turn left on the road toward the park registration building and retrieve your car. This loop takes approximately three hours and is a good introduction to the desert.

THE RINCON MOUNTAINS

*R*incón means *corner* in Spanish. It is not known for certain how the mountain range to the east got its name. Topped by the 8,666-foot Mica Mountain, the Rincons have historically been the least accessible of the four ranges around Tucson.

Hohokam Indians camped and lived in the Rincons, as they did in the Santa Catalina and the Tucson Mountains. In Box Canyon, five bedrock mortars show where Indian women ground legumes. Petroglyphs adorn rocks and cliffs. When the Hohokam left, the mountains were generally free of human habitation until the early 1800s, when the Apache wandered into the range. The mining that led to the development of the other ranges was almost nonexistent in the Rincons.

By the late 1800s the lower areas of the Rincons saw extensive ranching. The Tanque Verde Guest Ranch at the end of Speedway was once the ranch of Emilio Carrillo. Carrillo's and other ranchers' cattle grazed in the foothills of the Rincons, trampling small saguaros. Lime kilns that were operated in the 1880s used twelve cords of wood at each firing, the gathering of which seriously deforested the area. The remains of these kilns can be seen along the Cactus Forest Trail.

The Rincons were as cool and attractive as the Santa Catalinas, but few people took advantage of their heights. One who did was Levi Manning, a mayor of Tucson and former surveyor general of the United States. He discovered a flat area at about 8,000 feet near Mica Mountain and decided to homestead the area. In preparation for this, he had Mexican laborers build a wagon road to the site, and he constructed a large log cabin. For a few years Manning Camp was the social center of Tucson in the summer months. He even hauled a piano to the site. However, his homestead application had not been approved when the Rincon Mountains became part of the Coronado National Forest, and it was declared void. Manning abandoned the camp and never returned.

The Forest Service began using the cabin and the site in the early 1920s to set up a permanent fire-control center. The camp has been spruced up with modern conveniences and additional bunkhouses over the years. Maintaining the camp became too expensive, and in

1976 everything was dismantled except the original log cabin, which Manning built in the early 1900s. That cabin is still used by the staff of the Saguaro National Park when they are working in the area.

The foothills of the Rincons drew the attention of world-renowned ecologist and University of Arizona president Homer Shantz in the late 1920s. Shantz dreamed of preserving the magnificent stand of saguaros for use as a study area. Through his efforts the state did purchase the land, but when the depression hit, the state was unable to keep up the payments. Through a property transfer agreement, the federal government took over in 1933, establishing the Saguaro National Monument. Additional property was purchased from private individuals in the early 1970s. In 1939, a few years after the establishment of the monument, great numbers of the giant saguaros began to rot and die. Coincidentally, in February of that year the coldest temperatures ever recorded caused the mercury to fall to 25 degrees and remain there for several hours. At first, plant scientists did not make any connection between the low temperatures and the diseased plants. By 1941, so many saguaros were dying that the National Park Service removed diseased arms and buried whole plants that showed evidence of the rot. Plans were considered for transplanting young saguaros in the area. Before this was implemented, the policy of the National Park Service became more accepting of nature and did not interfere with the natural progression of plant life.

In the two decades that followed, extensive studies were conducted on the saguaro population. The studies led scientists to conclude that the freeze of 1939 had weakened the old giant saguaros by making them susceptible to the bacterial infection, and that the demise of the saguaros was just part of the natural cycle in their long lives. Younger, stronger plants are able to fight off infection by forming a "boot," or callus, and sealing off the disease from the rest of the plant.

An attack of a different kind occurred in the mid-1950s. The National Park Service drew up plans to develop the Rincon Mountains in a manner similar to the Mount Lemmon area. A 19-mile road called the Desert Mountain Highway would be constructed from the monument headquarters to Manning Camp. The thinking at the time was that such development would relieve the stress on the Mount Lemmon area, and that the rapid growth of the Tucson area demanded more recreational facilities. Fortunately for hikers who enjoy the wilderness, the Desert Mountain Highway never materialized.

In 1994, the status of the Saguaro National Monument changed, and today it is known as Saguaro National Park.

Reaching the highlands of the Rincons requires backpacking. Unlike the trails in the Santa Catalinas, which steeply and quickly ascend into the high country, the trails in the Rincon Mountains traverse many miles of foothills before reaching the ponderosa pine level.

Because this guide is restricted to hikes that can be completed in one day, I have included only five hikes in the Rincon Mountains. One is an exceptionally easy trek along the Cactus Forest Trail. A second easy hike climbs Pink Hill and goes to Little Wild Horse Tank. The Douglas Spring and Tanque Verde Ridge Trails are long but relatively easy hikes across the foothills to about the 6,000-foot level. The only hike I have included that gets you into the high country is the hike to Rincon Peak.

Cactus Forest Trail

General Description: *A basically flat ramble across the desert, through many varieties of cacti and past some old lime kilns*

Difficulty: *Easy*

Best Time of Year to Hike: *Winter, late fall, early spring*

Length: *10.4 miles, round-trip*

Miles to Trailhead from Speedway/Campbell Intersection: *13.9 miles*

Directions to Trailhead from Speedway/Campbell Intersection: *Go south on Campbell to the intersection of Broadway. Turn east (left) on Broadway, following it until a sign indicates 1.5 miles to the dead end of Broadway. About 0.2 mile beyond the sign, a parking area on the right indicates the beginning of Cactus Forest Trail.*

The Cactus Forest Trail meanders across the desert from Broadway Boulevard to Old Spanish Trail and is a good introduction to the lowlands of the Rincon Mountains. The ideal way to hike this trail is to leave a vehicle at the trailhead parking area on Old Spanish Trail and begin the hike from the Broadway trailhead.

I recommend stopping at the Saguaro National Park Visitor Center at the intersection of Freeman Road and Old Spanish Trail to pick up the brochure showing the Cactus Forest Trail System before hiking this trail. A small trail sign marks the beginning of the Cactus Forest Trail. Follow the arrow to the left 0.1 mile to the intersection of the Shantz Trail. Again, follow the arrow pointing in the direction of the Cactus Forest Trail.

The smooth, sandy trail passes many old, giant saguaros. Although palo verde and mesquite trees "nurse" a number of young saguaros here, this area is primarily an aging saguaro forest. The saguaro and an abundance of other cactus varieties make the name Cactus Forest Trail appropriate.

For most of the trail there is little elevation gain or loss. Mostly

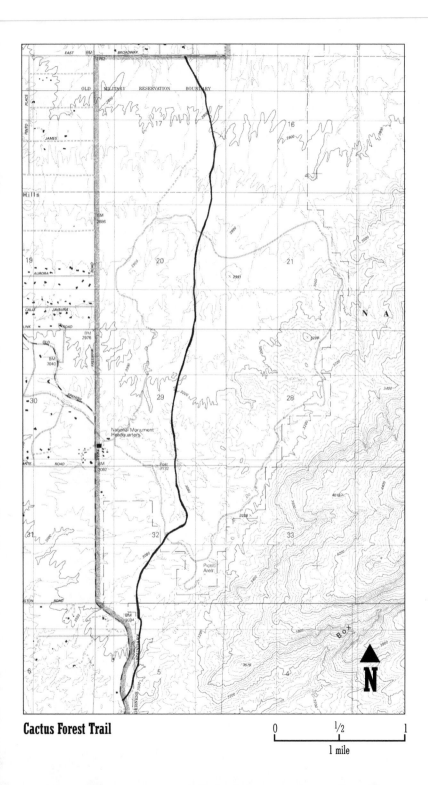

Cactus Forest Trail

0   ½   1

1 mile

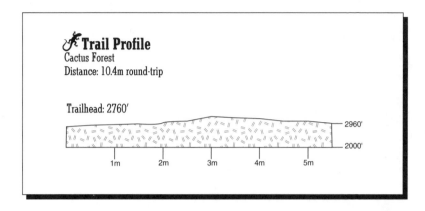

ᘓ **Trail Profile**
Cactus Forest
Distance: 10.4m round-trip

Trailhead: 2760'

level, the trail drops in and out of several small drainages and occasionally crosses a sandy wash. At 0.7 of a mile a sign indicates the intersection of the Cholla Trail. If you want a brief look at this area, the Cholla Trail makes a 2.1-mile loop with the Loma Verde/Mesa Trails and rejoins the Cactus Forest Trail. To stay on the main Cactus Forest Trail, continue straight ahead. This section has many creosote bushes. If you rub a few leaves and smell your fingers, you will realize why it is called creosote, even though the plant has no connection with the actual substance. In early spring the tiny yellow flowers of the creosote bush make a showy display.

You will note that there are several side trails leading off the main trail. Always continue straight ahead, avoiding any side trails. As you hike this trail, see how many small saguaro you can spot. Because this area was heavily grazed in earlier years, there are very few remaining small saguaro. It will take well over one hundred years before this may once again be a "cactus forest."

As you approach the paved road of Saguaro National Park East, you see a small hill to the left called Observatory Hill. When this area was owned by the University of Arizona, there was some discussion about building an observatory on this hill and the top was leveled, but the property was acquired by the federal government before any such plans materialized. Beside the drive is a sign for the Cactus Forest trailhead, at which point you will have come 1.8 miles. Cross the road in the painted crosswalk and continue the trail on the other side. Bicycles are permitted on this section between the paved road segments. In a few hundred yards you pass some concrete foundations on the right. This was the location of the park's first ranger station.

Lime kilns first used in the 1880s, Cactus Forest Trail

Nine-tenths of a mile from Cactus Forest Drive are the lime kilns, large beehive structures to the left and below the trail. A sign explains that these kilns were constructed around 1880. Limestone was brought down from the nearby hills and heated to a very high temperature to form lime. The lime was used to produce mortar and whitewash. Each batch of lime burned about twelve cords of wood from nearby trees. Carmen Moreno operated the kilns from 1914 to 1917, selling lime to Tucson building contractors for $10 a ton. This lime was used in the construction of the rock wall around the University of Arizona. In 1920, ranchers forced the closure of the kilns because of the destruction of cattle forage. A warning that bee colonies now inhabit the kilns is not needed, because the bees themselves prohibit close inspection of the kilns. Also, once, when I leaned over to take a picture of one of the kilns, a huge rattler encouraged me on my way! The kilns are an important part of the history of this area and should be left undisturbed.

Right past the kilns is a sign that says, "Dead End Trail." This is an easy 0.4-mile jaunt to Lime Falls. Thinking that I would find a waterfall, I took the side trip. Although the trail does drop into a large wash and through a thick mesquite forest, my hope of finding water was not realized. It is a pretty area, however, and at the correct time of day, as evidenced by the large number of deer and javelina footprints, your chances of seeing wildlife would be excellent.

Past the dead-end trail sign, the Cactus Forest Trail goes through an area with very few cacti. A low gray-green shrub and short grasses predominate. Here the trail begins to climb slightly for the first time, going up and down a series of small hills, making a nice change. The sweeping views of the surrounding mountain ranges are dramatic.

As the trail nears West Cactus Forest Drive, there are many side trails that can be confusing, again as a result of the large number of horseback riders in the area. Continue straight ahead. The trail is wide and sandy at this point. To the left is a large wash that has cut quite a swath in times of heavy runoff. There are many large mesquite trees. It is in this area that the great horned owls breed. The trail becomes an old road in this area, and again there are very few cacti, just a few prickly pears and chollas.

The trail crosses West Cactus Forest Drive and continues 0.9 of a mile to Old Spanish Trail. Hopefully you will have left a vehicle in the parking area. Otherwise, it's 5.2 miles back to the Broadway trailhead.

Pink Hill–Wentworth–
Loma Verde Loop Trail

General Description: *A hike to a rugged canyon, past a dam and across an old airstrip*

Difficulty: *Moderate, some areas of steep climbing*

Best Time of Year to Hike: *Winter, early spring, late fall*

Length: *8 miles, Pink Hill–Wentworth–Loma Verde Loop*

Miles to Trailhead from Speedway/Campbell Intersection: *13.9 miles*

Directions to Trailhead from Speedway/Campbell Intersection: *Go south on Campbell to the intersection of Broadway Boulevard. Turn east (left) on Broadway, following it until a sign indicates 1.5 miles to the dead end of Broadway. About 0.2 mile beyond the sign, a parking area on the right is signed as the Broadway Trailhead. The Pink Hill–Wentworth–Loma Verde Loop Trail begins 0.2 mile to the left of the small trail sign.*

Wild Horse Canyon is a rugged and beautiful canyon that can be reached by using a combination of the Shantz, Pink Hill, Squeeze Pen, Carrillo, and Wild Horse Trails. Pink Hill is a small, cone-shaped hill 1.6 miles from the trailhead. So named because the iron oxide content of the soil makes it pink, the hill is barely noticeable from the desert floor. However, as you ascend the trail and are able to look down on the hill, it stands out as a definite pink hill. After reaching Wild Horse Canyon, we will return to the trailhead via the Wild Horse, Wentworth, Loma Verde, Pink Hill, and Shantz Trails.

I have to admit that this trail is my nemesis. It is the reason I first wrote this hiking guide in 1990. At that time, there was a beautiful pool, known as Little Wild Horse Tank, in Wild Horse Canyon, containing hundreds of goldfish of varying sizes and colors. I undertook a hike with a friend and my son to show them the goldfish and got hopelessly

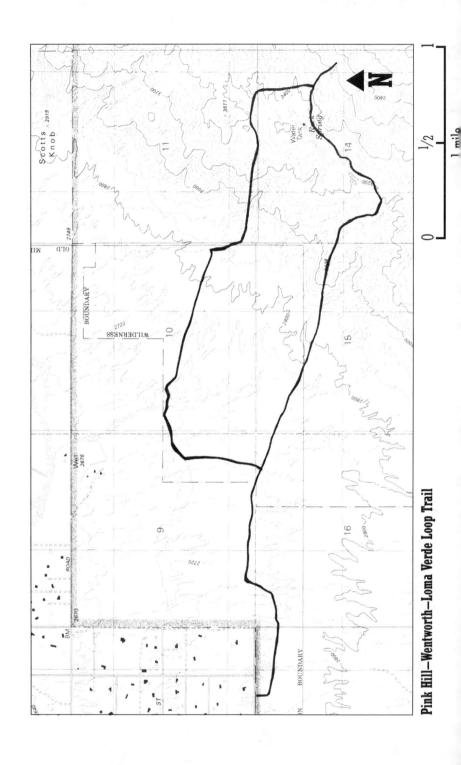

Pink Hill–Wentworth–Loma Verde Loop Trail

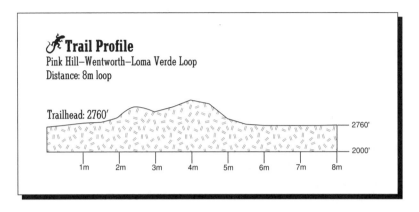

✒ **Trail Profile**
Pink Hill–Wentworth–Loma Verde Loop
Distance: 8m loop

Trailhead: 2760′

2760′

2000′

1m   2m   3m   4m   5m   6m   7m   8m

entangled in a maze of unmarked trails. We finally found the goldfish, but, as penance, I re-hiked the trail and wrote a detailed description, thus, the beginning of my "career" as a writer of hiking guides.

It would be wonderful if I could say that this was the end of my confusion on this trail. Unfortunately, that is not true. Even after the National Park Service placed new signs at every turn, I still got turned around. In the fall of 1995, a friend and I set out to double-check all directions, and, you guessed it, we turned right where we should have turned left and added an extra mile to the hike. We went back, double-checked it again, and I am now convinced that what follows is the definitive guide to the Pink Hill–Wentworth–Loma Verde Loop. These instructions, plus a copy of "Day Hiking Trails of the Rincon Mountain District," available at the Saguaro National Park East District Visitor Center, should get you there and back without a wrong turn.

As you must realize by the number of trails already mentioned, you work your way through a maze enroute to Wild Horse Canyon. The trails, which were created by the many horseback riders who frequent the area, have been made less confusing by the new signs. Unfortunately, the signs themselves are a bit confusing. The trail you are currently on is written at the top of the sign in capital letters and has no directional arrow. Trails that cut off the main trail are indicated in smaller letters, with an arrow indicating the direction to turn.

A small sign indicates the trails. Turn left, following the Shantz Trail for 0.1 mile to the intersection of the Shantz Trail and the Cactus Forest Trail. Follow the arrow to the Pink Hill Trail. As you stand facing the sign, PINK HILL TRAIL is written at the top of the sign and does not have a directional arrow. This indicates, as I endeavored to explain, that the Pink Hill Trail is straight ahead, or the trail on which you will be hiking.

Let's hope you are not already confused! Here's the scenario. You've turned left at the trailhead, turned left on the Shantz Trail, and are hiking along on the Shantz Trail, when you come to the intersection of the Pink Hill Trail. Now turn right, toward the Rincon mountains to the east. Voilà! The trail crosses several small washes before coming to a deeper, more pronounced wash. Just past this wash, a trail intersection sign marks the meeting of the Loma Verde and Pink Hill Trails. Remember it, because this is where you will rejoin the Pink Hill Trail on your return.

The Pink Hill Trail goes straight ahead, again toward the mountains, and climbs Pink Hill. It is a rocky, fairly steep, but short, climb to the top. This is a favorite destination for horseback riders, and the top is practically barren of vegetation. There are excellent views of the Santa Catalina and Tucson Mountains and most of the city of Tucson. As you look toward the Rincons, you can see Wild Horse Canyon and the old wagon road climbing the side of the mountain into the canyon.

The Saguaro Trail turns left off of Pink Hill, but your route is straight ahead, down the hill toward the mountains, and across a deep wash to the intersection of the Squeeze Pen Trail. Turn right on Squeeze Pen Trail. For approximately 0.2 of a mile you will head south, parallel to the Rincons. When you reach the Carrillo Trail intersection, turn left, and you are again heading toward the mountains.

For about 0.2 of a mile the Carrillo Trail meanders along the side of and then across a large drainage, which is the drainage out of Wild Horse Canyon. Most of the year there is some water in the wash, which has lush vegetation with reeds growing in the pools. In early spring this is a good place to find wildflowers.

Across the wash, the trail climbs gradually out and bears left. After a few steps you get your first views of Garwood Dam. The dam is a large concrete structure that crosses the lower portion of Wild Horse Canyon. It is slightly to the right and across the base of the mountain. This dam was built as a water supply in the 1940s by a rancher named Nelson Garwood. A small room at the base of the dam was used to store equipment. Garwood's house was located on a flat area near the dam.

Enroute to the dam you will pass cutoffs for the Deer Valley, Kennedy, and Freight Wagon Trails. When you reach the intersection of the Garwood Trail, turn right on the old wagon road that leads to

Hiker sitting on edge of Garwood Dam, Pink Hill–Wentworth–Loma Verde Loop Trail

Garwood Dam. This is still the Carrillo Trail. As you round the curve in the road, look below on the right. There are large pools of water, and most of the year there is some water flowing. When you reach the dam, you will be surprised at the size of the structure. It is tempting, but unsafe, to walk across the dam.

Past the dam, the trail climbs to the left. This portion of the trail has the steepest elevation gain, but the segment is short and near Little Wild Horse Tank. The trail quickly reaches the intersection of the Wild Horse Trail. At the intersection, turn right, through two fence posts, into Wild Horse Canyon. Most of the year the stream is flowing and will require wading or boulder-hopping to cross.

Across the canyon, the correct route is up the hill and to the left. Part way up, a trail forks to the left to go down to the creek. Ignore it and continue on up the hill for 100 yards, before bearing left down into what is known as Little Wild Horse Tank. This is all that remains of a once lovely, deep pool filled with goldfish. It was a secret pool, known only to the most dedicated of hikers and horseback riders. Because the fish were not native, the Forest Service removed them.

This action would not have been necessary, because, after the Chiva Fire, which destroyed 9,580 acres in the summer of 1989, a heavy rain dumped tons of sand and gravel into the pool, filling it to near capacity and leaving no room for goldfish. Little Wild Horse Tank has been reduced to a small pool at the base of the falls and that is only during the rainy season. It is still, however, a lovely spot and worth the hike to see the rugged country where wild horses may have once roamed.

To return, retrace your steps across the drainage, again going through the fence posts. Follow the Wild Horse Trail straight ahead. This is a pretty area, going in and out of small drainages that have a large number of small saguaros. Just past the intersection of Three Tank Trail, the Wild Horse Trail bears left and begins the descent out of the foothills. The view of the Tucson valley spreads out below. Look on the desert floor slightly to the right, and you will see a green area that was once a landing strip. This is our eventual goal, but for now, look to the left for a deep chasm cut by the force of water. Deep, dark pools have led to this section being called the "Black Hole." Past the pools, the trail drops rather steeply and then flattens out and becomes a smooth, easy trail.

When you reach the desert floor, watch for signs pointing to the Wentworth Trail. It is a major intersection with three signs and can be confusing. The correct route is to remain on the Wildhorse Trail, which goes directly north toward the Catalinas. After 0.2 of a mile, at another signed intersection, the Wentworth Trail turns left and soon joins the landing strip. Notice that there are no saguaros for the length of the strip, but there are large saguaros on either side. This strip belonged to Garwood, who had a small building here to house his private plane.

At the intersection of Wentworth and Kennedy Trails, continue straight ahead on Wentworth. You are now leaving the airstrip. Pass through two small fence posts, and in about 0.2 of a mile, you drop down into a wide wash. In the center of the wash, still another intersection sign indicates the meeting of the Saguaro and Wentworth Trails. Stay on Wentworth, which bears slightly to the right and follows the bottom of the wash. You will notice a fence on the right. The trail crosses a wide, sandy wash into a grassy area with a number of mesquite—a welcome respite from the sun.

At the Loma Verde Trail intersection you leave the Wentworth Trail and turn left. There is another sign in 0.1 of a mile. Keep bearing left on the Loma Verde Trail, to the intersection of the Pink Hill Trail.

Now you are back in familiar territory. Turn right on the Pink Hill Trail, to the intersection of Pink Hill Trail and Shantz Trail, then turn left for 0.3 of a mile, to the intersection of the Cactus Forest and Shantz Trails. Bear right for less than a tenth of a mile, and you'll see the trailhead.

If you made it through this maze without a wrong turn, treat yourself to a brew, and while you're at it, drink one for me! I have hiked this combination more times than I care to remember!

Tanque Verde Ridge Trail

General Description: *A long hike, mostly along the ridge line, through changing vegetation to the Juniper Basin Campground*

Difficulty: *Difficult, some areas of steep climbing*

Best Time of Year to Hike: *Winter, early spring, late fall*

Length: *13.8 miles, round-trip*

Miles to Trailhead from Speedway/Campbell Intersection: *11.5 miles to Visitor Center parking lot; 1 mile to Javelina picnic area*

Directions to Trailhead from Speedway/Campbell Intersection: *Go south on Campbell to the intersection of Broadway Boulevard. Turn east (left) on Broadway until the intersection of Old Spanish Trail. There is no light at this intersection. It is past the intersection of Pantano Road and before Camino Seco. Turn right on Old Spanish Trail to the entrance of Saguaro National Park East District. Enter the park (there is a $3 fee) and follow signs to the Javelina picnic area. A sign indicates the parking area for the Tanque Verde Ridge Trail.*

---

*T*anque verde, Spanish for *green tank,* is a name used often in the Rincon Mountains. There's a Tanque Verde wash, falls, canyon, ridge, peak, guest ranch, and, of course, hiking trail. Its use originated in the 1860s, when rancher William Oury tried to avoid Indian attacks on his cattle by moving the entire herd to the base of a ridge on the southeast corner of the Rincons. Two large waterholes (or tanks) containing green algae were on the range, and the area came to be referred to as Tanque Verde.

The Tanque Verde Trail follows Tanque Verde Ridge to Juniper Basin and on to Cowhead Saddle, where it connects with the Cowhead Saddle Trail to continue the climb to Manning Camp. The section of the trail that ends at Juniper Basin makes an excellent, although long, day hike.

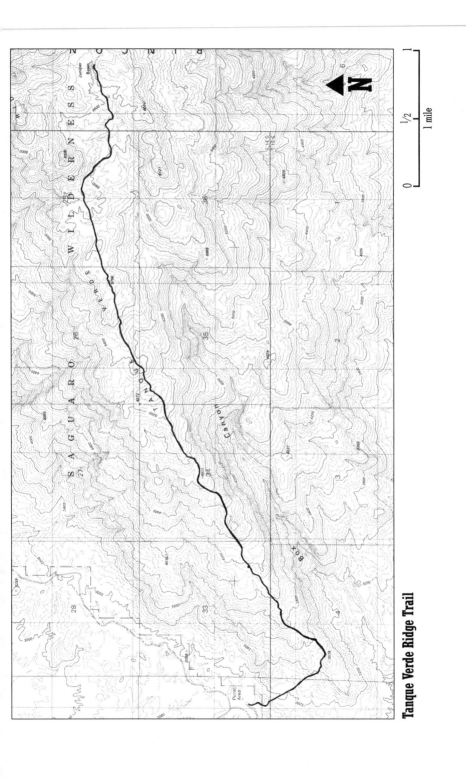

Tanque Verde Ridge Trail

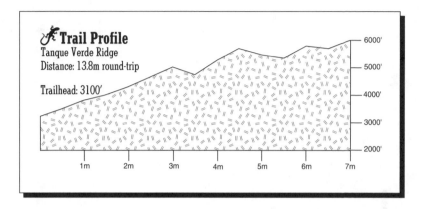

🦎 **Trail Profile**
Tanque Verde Ridge
Distance: 13.8m round-trip

Trailhead: 3100'

The trail begins to the right of the Javelina Picnic Area. It goes slightly downhill and crosses a small drainage, before beginning to climb. There are many cacti in this area, including several large, healthy saguaros. Past another small drainage is a trail register.

After the trail register the climb is steeper, and you quickly come to a good lookout point, from which you can see the telescopes on Kitt Peak and most of the southern part of Tucson. After this lookout point, the trail levels out and is smooth and sandy for a short distance, before it drops into another drainage. As the trail climbs out of this drainage, the climb increases and the views get better. You can see all of Tucson and, on a clear day, as far north as Picacho Peak. Occasionally there is a faint side trail where hikers have gone for a better view, or the trail crosses rock slabs, making the correct route somewhat confusing. Take your time, look for cairns, and avoid stepping over a row of rocks intended to stop you from taking the wrong trail. For the most part, the Tanque Verde Ridge Trail is easy to follow, and if you do go astray momentarily, it is always possible to backtrack and find the correct route.

The first part of the trail follows a pattern of crossing small drainages and leveling out for awhile, with the views of the valley ever improving. After about 1-1/2 miles you top out on the ridge, and you can see why the name Tanque Verde Ridge Trail is justified. Most of the trail from here on follows the ridge line, going to either the north or south, but always coming back to the ridge. The views from the ridge are spectacular. To the south in the Santa Ritas are Mount Wrightson and Mount Hopkins. Ahead and to the southeast is Rincon

View of Tucson from the Tanque Verde Ridge Trail

Peak. To the west are the Tucson Mountains, and to the north, a magnificent view of the Santa Catalinas. Some fire damage remains in this area—the result a motor vehicle-ignited fire in the summer of 1995.

The vegetation is typical of this elevation. Saguaro, prickly pear, cholla, ocotillo, and hedgehog make this area especially pretty in mid-April when the cacti bloom. As you leave the ridge line and begin to circle the hill to the north, there is a deep drainage on the left. Along this section of the trail is a small sign that indicates that you have reached the 4,000-foot elevation level. Past the sign is a drainage that occasionally has small pools of water, especially after a summer rain. There are long stretches of flat, easy walking, with only slight elevation gain. Rarely do you find a shady spot. The views continue to be great, and this would be an excellent place to hike to see the sunset and then the lights of the city at night.

Also, past the 4,000-foot sign, the saguaros become scarce, and a few varieties of oak begin to appear. There is a large section covered with bear grass. Bear grass is used today by Tohono O'odham basket makers. Many years ago, the sharp-edged grass was used by the Apaches to cut off the noses of women accused of adultery.

An interesting feature of this hike is the opportunity to observe the changing vegetation that accompanies the increase in elevation. Past the section covered with bear grass, the first juniper and piñon pines begin to appear. The trail occasionally tops out on the ridge, levels out for a distance, and then drops to the north or south side of the ridge. The views are amazing, and this is one of the best parts of the Tanque Verde Trail, because it has views in all directions.

About 2 miles past the 4,000-foot marker, you come to another sign that indicates a 5,000-foot elevation. From here, it takes almost two hours to reach the campground. By now there are no saguaros. The vegetation is mainly several varieties of oak, juniper and piñon pine, and manzanita. The plant that I call the hiker's nemesis, amole, commonly known as shindaggers, begins to appear. Imagine how it would feel to tumble into a patch of amole!

You are now far back into the foothills of the Rincons, and the rest of the trail goes up and down small hills. As you progress into the foothills, the trees increase in density and size. As you continue along the trail, the city disappears, and the views are not as spectacular. You have the feeling of real isolation in this area.

After you drop into a narrow, sandy stream bed, you are about 1 mile from the Juniper Basin Campground. For a few hundred yards, there is a section of loose rock that makes the climb more difficult. Red metal strips are now on the trees to mark the trail so that it can be followed in snow.

Soon the trail crosses a wide, flat, rocky area. Several large cairns mark the correct route. Across the rocks, the trail goes along the side of a drainage and is a pretty area. The trees are much larger now. You then cross a stream bed, with an unusual dark gray rock bottom. A few hundred yards past this stream bed is the Juniper Basin Campground.

Reservations must be made at park headquarters for overnight camping. There are picnic tables, grills, and a rest room at the campground. The area is covered with exceptionally large juniper, the bark of which looks much like the skin of an alligator, thus, the common name of the tree is alligator juniper. The elevation at the campground is 6,000 feet.

Hiking time to the campground is four to five hours, with a little less time required for the return. Unless, that is, you happen to be carrying heavy backpacks, as did the three volunteer rangers we found camped at Juniper Basin on our last hike into this area. Rick Collins, Roger Carrillo, and Jeff Coleman were spending several days at the campground, doing trail and campground maintenance and removing pink tags left by an extensive search and rescue operation the previous summer. Should you be interested in becoming a volunteer ranger, stop by the Saguaro National Park Visitor Center on your return for information. The "three C's," as they call themselves, seemed to be enjoying their work and even invited us to stop by for dinner. But, alas, we couldn't accept. We had 6.9 miles to go before dark!

Douglas Spring Trail

General Description: *A hike to Douglas Spring Campground, through an area recovering from a major fire that happened in the summer of 1989*

Difficulty: *Difficult*

Best Time of Year to Hike: *Winter, early spring, late fall*

Length: *11.8 miles, round-trip*

Miles to Trailhead from Speedway/Campbell Intersection: *15 miles*

Directions to Trailhead from Speedway/Campbell Intersection: *Go east on Speedway until it dead-ends. Turn right to the trailhead parking area.*

The Douglas Spring Trail crosses the foothills of the Rincon Mountains to the Douglas Spring Campground. Past the campground the trail continues to Cowhead Saddle and serves as a connecting trail for several loops used by backpackers. Much of the vegetation on the last 6 miles of the trail was consumed by the Chiva Fire in the summer of 1989. Hiking this area today provides an example of the benefits of a fire. New growth covers most of the fire-damaged area.

A lightning strike on July 5, 1989, started a fire near the northern boundary of Saguaro National Park. The fire burned 9,580 acres before it was controlled on July 10, including the entire Douglas Spring Campground and much of the Douglas Spring Trail. After being closed for revegetation and rehabilitation for nearly ten months, the trail was reopened in April 1990. Today the trail is in excellent condition and is always easy to follow.

A sign at the trailhead describes the Manning Camp Trail system. This description will include that portion of the trail to Douglas Spring Campground. After 0.1 of a mile there is a trail register, and, as you can see by the number of signatures, this is a popular trail, especially on weekends. The first half mile of the trail is nearly level and passes

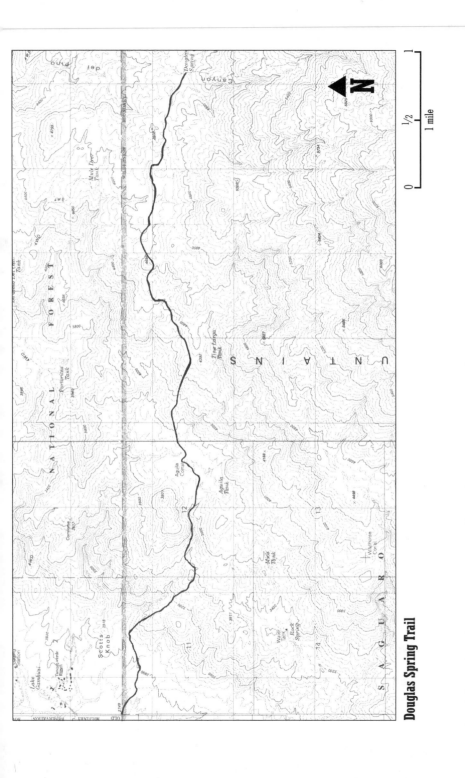

Douglas Spring Trail

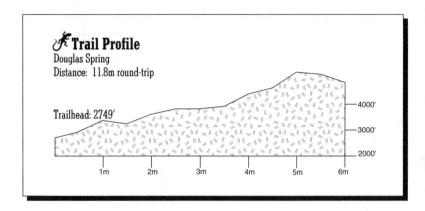

Trail Profile
Douglas Spring
Distance: 11.8m round-trip

Trailhead: 2749′

through saguaro, prickly pear, barrel, and cholla cacti, ocotillo, and palo verde and mesquite trees. You will notice that there are very few small saguaros. Before becoming a preserved area, this section was heavily used by ranchers, and many small saguaros were trampled by cattle. At 0.6 of a mile you come to the intersection of the Wentworth Trail. An excellent map of the intersecting trails in this area is available at the Saguaro National Park East District Visitor Center.

Past the intersection, the trail begins to climb gradually, and as you ascend, you see the pink buildings of the Tanque Verde Guest Ranch to the northeast and most of the Tucson valley. The Douglas Spring Trail goes to the left of the hill and begins to climb more steeply. To the left of the trail is a deep, rugged drainage. Most of the year there are pools of water and some water trickling over the rocks, making this an excellent spot to see wildlife, especially mule deer. As the trail climbs steeply around the hill, you will note that steps have been dug into the steeper sections, with rocks placed for erosion control. As you top the first hill, you come to a flat spot that is used frequently as a rest stop. You can see a trail beaten out to the top of the hill by hikers who wanted to see the view. There is no rush to do this, because there are several good viewing spots along the trail farther along.

There are many prickly pears along this trail. You may be surprised to learn that this common desert plant played an important part in world history. Look carefully on the prickly pear pads for a whitish, flaky substance that looks like artificial snow. This is actually a small insect—cochineal—that is the source of a brilliant red dye. When the

Hikers starting up the beautiful Douglas Spring Trail

Spanish explorer Cortez entered Mexico in 1519, he encountered Aztec men and women wearing dazzling red garments. On learning the source of the dye, Cortez arranged for prickly pear to be cultivated in Spain. For nearly three centuries, this was a closely guarded Spanish secret, so much so that the red cloth made from the dye became known as the "color of kings." Scrape a patch of cochineal with a stick and its tip will turn red, the color of kings.

From the flat spot the trail again begins to climb up the side of another hill, and by now the views of the city are excellent. Again there are good views of the drainage on the left. The trail continues to climb and switchback up the hill, flattens out for a short period, and then begins climbing again, this time along the right side of the hill. As you walk along the side of the hill, you'll see another drainage to the right. This frequently has water and is also a good spot to see wildlife. When I hiked this trail in early May I saw seven deer in this section. The trail climbs steeply for a short distance then once again levels out, continuing to follow the drainage.

From this point on, fire damage was extensive. When I hiked this trail in April 1990, prickly pears lay in heaps of discarded charcoal, ocotillo stalks looked like burned hot dog-roasting sticks, and many tall saguaros were blackened skeletons. Today, the recovery is remarkable. Tall native grasses cover the ground, and, if you didn't know it, you could never tell this area had been burned just a few years ago.

The trail crosses several small drainages but continues to follow to the left of the main drainage for a quarter of a mile, before turning away and gradually climbing another small hill and then traversing a long flat area. In this flat area you have good views of the inner foothills. Large drainages come down. At the intersection of the Three Tank Trail, note that there are 3.6 miles to go before reaching the Douglas Spring Campground.

There are several small drainages before crossing a wide, sandy drainage that comes down from a steep, rocky section known as Bridal Wreath Falls. The tall, green mesquite trees in the low basin below the falls were totally missed by the fire. A side trail leads off to the right, and you might like to take time and explore this green area and the falls. It is especially beautiful in early spring, when snowmelt creates a large waterfall.

Past this green area the trail begins to climb again, this time quite steeply, before rounding a knoll and continuing to follow the drainage, which is by now a wide, sandy creek. In the drainage is what remains of a human-made wall. This is noted on the map as "Tina Larga Tank," and it contained water until being destroyed in the heavy rains of 1983.

As you continue to climb, the higher elevations of the Rincons stand out. The large outcropping of rocks straight ahead is Helen's Dome. A little farther east is Spud Rock, so named because a man of German descent retired from the railroad about 1890, moved into the Rincon Mountains, and raised potatoes near the rock.

After leaving the side of the hill, the trail rounds the hill, and you now begin a gradual decline into the Douglas Spring Campground, crossing in and out of several drainages, going up and down small hills, until reaching the campground. It is in this area that the fire was most intense, and where today, the damage is still most evident.

The campground, once an oasis of picnic tables and tall shade trees, is now composed of a rest room and signs indicating campsites. A few trees escaped the fire, but most of the shade is gone. There is still a spring, and water trickles over the rocks in the driest of seasons. If you've never been here before, you'll appreciate the solitude and enjoy watching birds fly among the dead trees—but if you remember the Douglas Spring Campground from before the fire, it's still too soon to go back. Give it another fifty years!

Rincon Peak Trail

General Description: *One of the most beautiful and difficult trails in the Rincon Mountains*

Difficulty: *Extremely difficult*

Best Time of Year to Hike: *Late spring, early fall, summer*

Length: *16.2 miles, round-trip, via Miller Creek Trail*

Miles to Trailhead from Speedway/Campbell Intersection: *57 miles*

Directions to Trailhead from Speedway/Campbell Intersection: *Go west on Speedway to I-10. Follow I-10 east to the Mescal exit. Turn left on Mescal Road for 16 miles. Mescal Road becomes Forest Service Road 35. At the intersection of FS 35 and FS 4407, a sign indicates that the Miller Creek trailhead is to the left. The trailhead is 0.2 of a mile from the sign. The first 3 miles of Mescal Road is paved. The rest, including FS roads, are unpaved but are suitable for passenger cars.*

Rincon Peak, at 8,482 feet, is the second highest point in the Rincon Mountain Range. The Miller Creek Trail, in combination with the Heartbreak Ridge and Rincon Peak Trails, is the shortest route to the summit. Although the Rincon Peak Trail is included in this guide as a day hike, one must be an exceptionally strong hiker to conquer this mountain in one day. If you plan to do so, I recommend that you drive to the trailhead the night before and begin your hike at daybreak.

The trail begins through a gate in the fence near the parking area. Markers indicate that this is part of the Arizona Trail System. The first few miles of the trail still show the effects of a fire that swept this area in the summer of 1995. The first part of the trail is basically level, crossing and recrossing Miller Creek several times. Most of the year there will be water in the stream, and the resultant vegetation makes for a pretty area. The sandy and smooth trail passes under large Arizona sycamores and Emory oaks and through manzanita. There are a few large barrel cacti that look out of place among this vegetation.

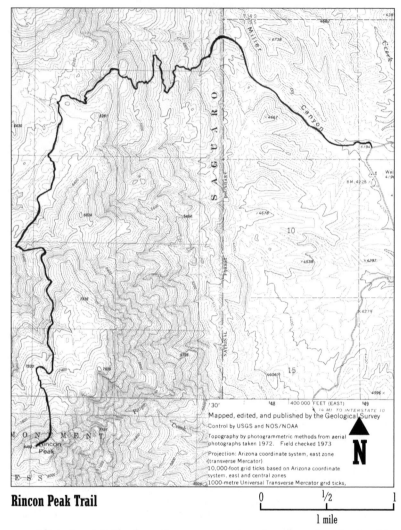

Rincon Peak Trail

After about 3/4 of a mile you come to a large pool and a jumble of rocks. Here you cross Miller Creek and then go to the left of a small drainage. The trail then begins to climb gradually, leaving the drainage and veering to the right, climbing more steeply for 200 yards, before dropping again into and crossing another drainage.

Immediately across this drainage is a fence and signs marking the boundary of the Saguaro National Park. There is a walk-through

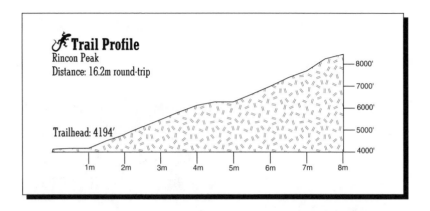

🦎 **Trail Profile**
Rincon Peak
Distance: 16.2m round-trip

Trailhead: 4194'

8000'
7000'
6000'
5000'
4000'

1m 2m 3m 4m 5m 6m 7m 8m

opening in the fence. The trail goes through a thick stand of manzanita, is sandy and rocky, and goes down and crosses a big boulderstrewn drainage. Across the drainage, the trail climbs steeply. Although there will be some pleasant, level stretches, basically, the easy part of this trail is over. There are places where the trail splits, but it comes back to the same place, so don't worry that you may make a wrong turn. The trail becomes very steep, with some high step-ups.

As you gain in elevation, the views of the surrounding mountains and valleys give you a forecast of the views to come. Vegetation changes to include alligator juniper and several varieties of oak.

After a seemingly endless climb through the manzanita and around boulders, the trail changes abruptly, turning left and dropping down into an exceptionally pretty area. It reaches a deep drainage and then climbs gradually along the left side of the drainage. Much of the year water is flowing in this area. The trail is covered by a canopy of trees. Grapevines here remind me of the eastern mountains, where as children we cut the vine and swung far out over ravines. Halfway up the drainage, a large pile of rocks makes an excellent lunch spot. In spring, wild geraniums and other flowers add to the beauty.

Near the head of the drainage on the right is the first ponderosa pine, the first of many to come. Past the ponderosa, the trail turns to the right and crosses a small drainage, before turning left and away from the large ravine. Here you begin to climb steeply again, and the canopy is gone as the view opens up, and the trail approaches Happy Valley Saddle. At the saddle, you get a good view of your goal, Rincon

Hiker sitting on the area's largest cairn on the summit of Rincon Peak

Peak. It really doesn't look possible that you can be on top of this mountain in a few miles.

At the saddle the trail drops slightly to the intersection of the Miller Creek Trail and the Heartbreak Ridge Trail. Turn left at this intersection 0.5 of a mile to the Rincon Peak Trail sign. Here you will turn left for the final 3.2 miles to the top of Rincon Peak. It takes three to five hours to reach this point.

An interesting side trip and an excellent spot for camping, should you decide to do this trail as a backpack, is to continue 1/4 of a mile past the Rincon Peak Trail intersection, to the Happy Valley Campground. The campground has three sites that must be reserved through the Saguaro National Park East District. It also has a grill, picnic tables, and rest room facilities. A stream runs through the campground and almost always has at least small pools of water. Tall ponderosas shade the area and carpet the ground with needles. Happy Valley Campground is truly one of the gems of the Rincons.

We'll assume that you are doing this trail as an all-out day effort and continue 3.2 miles up the Rincon Peak Trail to the summit. Past the intersection, the trail climbs slightly and then levels off. For nearly a mile the trail drops into and out of a series of small ravines. There are many alligator junipers and the ever-present manzanitas. The trail is still pleasant, and you may wonder where the difficult part is—don't worry, it will come soon enough. As the trail begins to climb, it crosses one large side drainage and, shortly, another one. Most of the year there will be some water trickling down the rocks in these drainages. By now you are in the open, where the views are astounding. Walk past a particularly thick stand of manzanitas, and you can see the western end of the city of Tucson. As you climb, more and more of the city will be visible. Past this point the trail begins to climb more steeply, with occasional switchbacks and some long, steep climbs. The views are always excellent. As you look toward Tucson, you can see Tanque Verde Ridge and catch a glimpse of the Catalina Mountains.

The trail drops in and out of several deep ravines. By now you are in ponderosa country. Along the side of the mountain you come to a small spring. A circle of rocks contains the actual spring, and the area surrounding the spring is covered with tiny, green clover-like plants. Past the spring you see the first Douglas fir. This is a beautiful section, not too steep, under a canopy of ponderosa pine and Douglas fir trees. The trail is soft and the climb imperceptible for a short distance. This cannot last if you are to reach the top.

Less than a mile from the summit, you reach a sign that says, "Foot Trail Only, No Stock." This sign marks the beginning of the final ascent on the peak. Be consoled by the views, which are spectacular, as you stop to rest on the way. It is steep, there are some switchbacks, but not enough for my liking. The trail is slippery, often covered with fallen branches and trees. A small patch of aspen grows near the top, one of the few stands of aspen in the Rincons. But persevere and you will make it. Near the top you actually go down a few steps, and there on a shelf is the trail register. You can see by the small number of signatures that not too many people make it to this point.

Unfortunately, this is not the top. There are 200 more yards of steep rock scrambling until you reach the summit. The trail is not always distinct in this section, but the only way is up. Work your way carefully from rock to rock, and you'll be there quickly.

The top is worth the climb, and on a clear day, you can truly see forever. It takes the average hiker two to three hours to do the final 3.2 miles. Not much grows on the top. A few manzanitas and, surprisingly, a number of hedgehog cacti. The wind can be very strong.

A cairn that is at least 10 feet high marks the actual summit. A summit register is anchored in a metal box near the summit. Should there be any sign of a storm, get off the summit. As you can imagine, this is a target for lightning. Hopefully you can remain here for a while and, with the aid of a map, pick out the mountain ranges you can see from here. If you are doing this as a day hike, don't linger too long. The way down is treacherous and takes almost as long as it did to come up.

THE SANTA CATALINA MOUNTAINS

In A.D. 900 Hohokam women ground mesquite beans in summer camps high in the canyons of the Santa Catalina Mountains, while their men hunted. Bedrock mortars and petroglyphs remain as evidence of their time in the mountains.

The Hohokam were gone and the Pima Indians were living in the Tucson basin by the time the Jesuit priest, Father Kino, established his mission at San Xavier del Bac in the late 1600s. Kino referred to the mountains to the north and east as the Santa Catarina Mountains, possibly in honor of Saint Catherine's Day. In time this changed to the Santa Catalina Mountains . . . the Catalinas.

By the early 1800s, Apache Indians hunted and camped in the Catalinas and occasionally raided the settlements and the mission near Tucson. To protect their missions and route to California, the Spaniards built a fort on the site of what is today downtown Tucson. Apaches attacked the fort unsuccessfully and the Spaniards survived, until the Mexican War of Independence shifted ownership of Tucson to Mexico in 1821.

By 1854, when the United States secured possession with the Gadsden Purchase, Anglos with the gleam of gold in their eyes began to move into Tucson. They built trails into the Catalinas, looking for gold, then silver and copper.

Others were interested in the Catalinas. Sara Plummer Lemmon and her husband came to the Catalinas in 1880. Botanists on their honeymoon, they rode horseback up from Oracle, guided by rancher E. O. Stratton. On the highest peak, the three carved their initials on a large pine and christened the peak Mount Lemmon, in honor of Sara. The name stuck, and today the 9,157-foot-high point of the Santa Catalinas is still called Mount Lemmon.

By 1891 there were those who thought these mountains should be protected, and Congress authorized the president to withdraw certain lands from the public domain. In 1902 the Catalina Forest Preserve was created. A conservationist president, Theodore Roosevelt, organized the National Forest Service in 1905, and by 1908 the Coronado National Forest was born.

More trails were built into the high country, and Tucsonans camped there in the summer. Some leased land and built cabins. Much discussion was devoted to building a road up the mountain. By 1920 a rough road had been carved up to the top from Oracle, but Tucsonans wanted a "short road" from their side of the mountain.

After much maneuvering by the then editor/publisher of the Tucson *Citizen,* Frank Hitchcock, Secretary of Agriculture Henry A. Wallace approved a 25-mile, two-lane, surfaced road up to the village of Summerhaven. The federal government would foot the bill, and the road would be built by prisoners. Construction began in 1933 and inched up the mountain. It was not completed until 1951. The road was named in honor of the man who got it all going, but who did not live to see it completed.

To protect the mountains from further development, in 1978 the Pusch Ridge Wilderness Area was created under the Endangered American Wilderness Act. In all, 56,933 acres, encompassing nearly the entire front range, are now closed to future development and all motorized vehicles. Mountain bikes are not permitted. The only way to get to the heart of this spectacular area is on foot or horseback.

There are eleven trails in the Catalinas described in this guide. I suggest starting with the first 3 miles of the Pima Canyon Trail for your first hike in the Catalinas. Follow this with the trek to Hutch's Pool out of Sabino Canyon and give Pontatoc Ridge a try. These three trails will introduce you to what I tritely continue to call the "magnificent" Santa Catalina Mountains.

West Fork of Sabino Trail
to Hutch's Pool

General Description: *A pleasant hike to one of the most beautiful pools in the Catalinas*

Difficulty: *Moderate, steep switchbacks for first 0.8 of a mile*

Best Time of Year to Hike: *Early spring, late fall, winter*

Length: *8.2 miles, round-trip, using the tram*

Miles to Trailhead from Speedway/Campbell Intersection: *11.1 miles*

Directions to Trailhead from Speedway/Campbell Intersection: *Go east on Speedway 5 miles to Wilmot Road. Turn left. Wilmot becomes Tanque Verde at the Pima intersection. Continue on Tanque Verde to Sabino Canyon Road. Turn left and follow the signs to the Sabino Canyon Visitor Center parking lot. The trailhead is 3.8 miles from the visitor center at the end of the Sabino Canyon Road. The Sabino Canyon tram goes to the trailhead.*

In the early 1940s Don Everett, English and Latin teacher at the Southern Arizona School for Boys (now Fenster School of Arizona), took his students on horseback rides into the Catalinas. Whenever he would pass a prominent landmark for the first time, Everett would name it after a student in his group. On a ride from Sabino Canyon to Mount Lemmon, Everett passed what he called "the most beautiful pool in the Catalinas." A student from Chicago, Roger Hutchinson, was on the ride, and Everett named the pool Hutch's Pool. It remains the most beautiful pool in the Catalinas.

The switchbacks at the north end of Sabino Canyon Road are the starting point for several trails leading into the Catalinas, including the West Fork of Sabino Trail, which passes Hutch's Pool. The quickest way

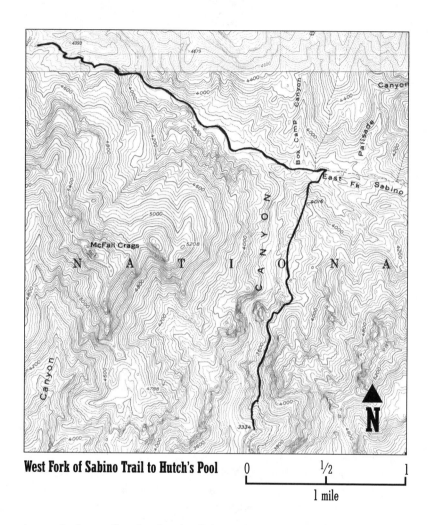

West Fork of Sabino Trail to Hutch's Pool

0   ¹/₂   1

1 mile

to reach the trailhead is by the Sabino Canyon tram ($5 per person); however, some hardy hikers prefer to walk the additional 3.8 miles to the switchbacks.

However you choose to traverse Sabino Canyon, you will agree that it is a rare oasis in the desert. No one knows for certain how Sabino Canyon got its name. David Wentworth Lazaroff, in his excellent book, *Sabino Canyon: The Life of a Southwestern Oasis*, theorizes that the name was applied by early Spanish-speaking visitors,

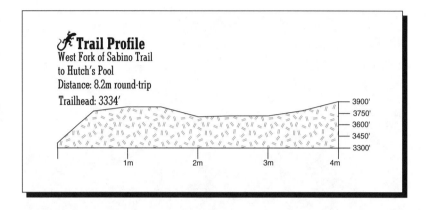

ⵌ Trail Profile
West Fork of Sabino Trail
to Hutch's Pool
Distance: 8.2m round-trip
Trailhead: 3334′

who often named places in Arizona after trees. He writes, "In Mexico 'sabino' is a name applied to small-fruited conifers such as bald cypress or juniper. The best candidate in Sabino Canyon is a beautiful tree called the Arizona cypress." He explains that although today only a few small cypress grow in the canyon, two hundred years ago the climate was wetter, and perhaps several large cypress grew near the mouth of the canyon, thus the name sabino, or cypress.

The trail to Hutch's Pool begins at the end of the road on the Sabino Canyon Trail and climbs steeply for 0.8 of a mile. After 0.5 of a mile, the Phoneline Trail cuts off to the right. This is a popular tram-hike loop for people who ride the tram up and hike the 4 miles back down the Phoneline Trail to lower Sabino Canyon.

After a few more switchbacks, the trail levels off along the top of the ridge. The city is now out of sight. To the left and far below is Sabino Creek. There are a few uphill, rocky spots, but for the most part, the trail is a gradual and easy climb until it begins meandering its way along the side of the ridge down to Sabino Basin.

After a mile and a half the trail makes a sharp curve to the right and begins descending quickly. At this curve, there is a partially barricaded side trail to the left leading to a lookout point, which provides an excellent view of Sabino Creek.

As you continue on the main trail and approach Sabino Basin, you can appreciate why it is such a popular area. A lush drainage, where Mexican blue oaks and Arizona sycamores flourish, the basin is a crossroads for hikers enroute to the backcountry of the Catalinas. From this point, it is 12 miles to Mount Lemmon, 2.5 miles back to

Hutch's Pool, West Fork of Sabino Trail to Hutch's Pool

Sabino Road, and 1.6 miles ahead to Hutch's Pool on the West Fork of Sabino Trail.

Blue jays claim this territory, and if you sit down for a snack or lunch, a jay will be observing to see if you drop a crumb. Toss one, and you'll hear the chatter of birds, and soon an entire flock will be sitting in the trees. Finally one gets brave enough to get the crumb, and the entire bunch heads after him.

When you tire of the jay performance and continue ahead to the pool, you first leave the drainage, cross a rocky, sandy area, and enter a meadow, hiking away from Sabino Creek for nearly a mile. A level, open field to the left is a popular campground. Archaeologists of the future could have a field day here, sifting through fire rings littered with the trash of the twentieth century. A quarter of a mile past the field, the trail begins to parallel Sabino Creek, going along a narrow ledge, where a slip could give you a pretty good tumble. Shortly, the trail descends into the drainage of, and then crosses, Sabino Creek. Although there are large boulders to hop on, the crossing could be treacherous in times of heavy runoff.

Cairns mark the trail, which now follows the left, or west, side of the creek. After a quarter of a mile, several paths to the right lead down to the creek. The first side trail leads to a large pool, which is a lovely spot but is not the actual Hutch's Pool. Continue ahead. The trail now bears left away from the stream for 0.2 of a mile. When the trail begins to climb slightly, look for a cairn in front of a large oak tree. A trail leads to the right, down to the stream to Hutch's Pool, which is long and narrow, with cliffs on each side and a waterfall at the north end.

It takes two to three hours to reach Hutch's Pool, depending on how long you linger along the way. If you care to explore a little farther, there are other smaller pools a few hundred yards upstream.

Blackett's Ridge Trail

General Description: *A short hike on a ridge between Sabino and Bear Canyons, with spectacular views of Tucson and the canyons*

Difficulty: *Moderate, steep for the first mile*

Best Time of Year to Hike: *Early spring, late fall, winter*

Length: *4.6 miles, round-trip*

Miles to Trailhead from Speedway/Campbell Intersection: *11.1 miles*

Directions to Trailhead from Speedway/Campbell Intersection: *Go east on Speedway 5 miles to Wilmot Road. Turn left. Wilmot becomes Tanque Verde at the Pima intersection. Continue on Tanque Verde to Sabino Canyon Road. Turn left and follow the signs to the Sabino Canyon Visitor Center parking lot. The trailhead can be reached by tram or by walking 0.8 of a mile across the desert and on the road (see text below).*

Blackett's Ridge is one of the best little hikes in the Tucson area. This ridge was named by Don Everett, a teacher at the Southern Arizona School for Boys, after one of his students. In 1937 Everett made the first ascent of the ridge on horseback, accompanied by Hill Blackett, Jr., a student from Winnetka, Illinois. From that day, the ridge has been called Blackett's Ridge.

You can reach the trailhead by riding the Bear Canyon tram, or, if you prefer, by walking on the wide path that crosses the desert from the east end of the Sabino Canyon parking lot. The trail starts between two brick pillars. When you reach the paved road, continue walking to the right, passing to the right of the rest rooms, across the bridge, and again to the right where a small sign on your left indicates several trails including the Blackett's Ridge Trail. If you are riding the tram, tell the driver that you want off at Stop 2, where you'll walk across the bridge and turn right to the trailhead. (To return by tram, you must be at the Stop 2 sign for pickup.)

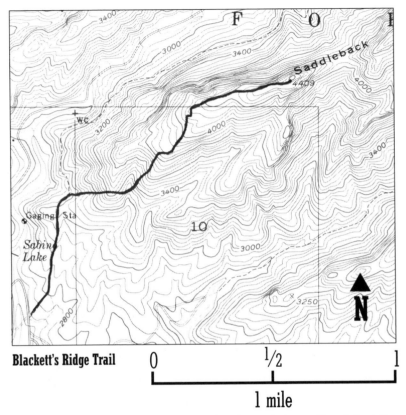

Blackett's Ridge Trail   0   ¹/₂   1

1 mile

After 100 yards, there is a signed trail intersection. Turn left at the intersection, following the Phoneline Trail to the cutoff for the Blackett's Ridge Trail. This trail follows the route of an old phone line to Mount Lemmon and is popular with joggers, who like to run up the trail and down the road, and with hikers, who ride the tram up Sabino Canyon and hike down the trail.

There is a very gradual elevation gain on smooth trail, through the typical vegetation of this elevation. After 0.4 of a mile you come to a signed turnoff to the right that leads to Blackett's Ridge. It takes about twenty minutes of leisurely hiking to reach this turnoff.

Straight ahead and high above is Blackett's Ridge. The Phoneline Trail continues up the canyon, and the trail to Blackett's Ridge begins

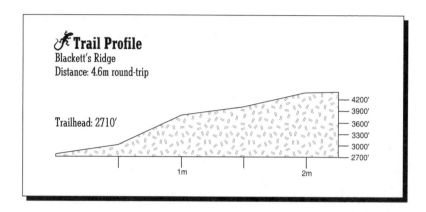

Trail Profile
Blackett's Ridge
Distance: 4.6m round-trip

Trailhead: 2710'

to switchback up the ridge. After about 1/4 of a mile, Sabino Canyon is visible, and you can see the tram. If the wind is right, you can hear the narration of the tram guide. Sabino Creek is visible, as is a small dam. In 1910 and again in the 1930s, private companies and government agencies made serious proposals to dam part of Sabino Canyon for use as Tucson's water and electric supply. Had any of these projects materialized, the views from Blackett's Ridge would be quite different!

The switchbacks become very steep and shorter as you come to the top of the front part of the trail. You level off briefly and wind around to the south side of the ridge. The Santa Ritas are now directly in front of you. In winter, which is the best time to do this hike, Mount Wrightson is usually snow covered, as are the Rincon Mountains to the east. As the trail continues, the switchbacks get even steeper, and soon the road leading to Bear Canyon is visible. A tram runs hourly to the popular Seven Falls Trailhead.

You quickly come to the first of several good lookout points. It is as if you were driving through the Rocky Mountains and come to signs saying, "Scenic Pullout." There are several such "pullouts" along the first part of this trail that are good places from which to sit and observe the valley below. You can easily make it to the first lookout in forty-five minutes.

As you recover from the steep climb, survey the sights. The greens of the Ventana Canyon golf course are in sharp contrast to the desert. By now, the parking lot of Sabino Canyon looks like a small asphalt square.

Blackett's Ridge

Past this first lookout, the trail continues gaining elevation. By the time you have reached the fourth lookout, you have an excellent view up Sabino Canyon and into the heart of the Catalinas. The towers on Radio Ridge stand out. The dark covering on top is ponderosa pine, another ecosystem altogether. You then come to a long, smooth saddle, and you know you are definitely on a narrow ridge between two canyons. On the right are the Rincons and Santa Ritas, and on the left are the Catalinas and Sabino Canyon.

As you cross the saddle, the trail again becomes rocky and climbs toward what looks like the high point of the ridge. Topped by a big pile of rocks, this high point is the first of three false summits. The trail is distinct and climbs gradually, going to the left of what appeared to be the high point.

As the trail ascends toward a second apparent summit, it bears slightly to the right and becomes quite steep. The area on the right was burned several years ago, and many of the saguaros show evidence of the fire. They are black around the bottom but still green at the top. They appear to be alive, but only time will tell if they will ultimately survive.

Straight ahead is a magnificent view of Thimble Peak; at 5,323 feet, it is the highest point in the canyon. The views from up here are great, but you do realize that the actual summit of Blackett's Ridge is still a few hundred yards ahead.

The trail ends abruptly. Climbing expertise is required for any further exploration of the ridge. Extreme caution must be exercised in this area. The cliffs to the left, called the Acropolis Cliffs by the tram drivers, drop 400 feet into Sabino Canyon. A misstep could be tragic.

However dangerous the summit of Blackett's Ridge, it does provide literally breathtaking views into Sabino Canyon. The Phoneline Trail has become a narrow ribbon. The now tiny-looking trams traverse the road, their drivers introducing tourists to the diversity of Sabino Canyon. As you sit quietly, you can hear the rush of water in Sabino Creek, occasionally mingled with the voices of people. Birds dive down the cliffs, and occasionally deer can be spotted as they head to the water below. The four mountain ranges surrounding Tucson make an unforgettable panorama.

It takes about an hour to return to the parking lot. The Blackett's Ridge hike is a good morning's workout, one that you will return to many times.

Esperero Trail

General Description: *A long hike over rugged terrain, with dramatic views of the Tucson valley*

Difficulty: *Extremely difficult*

Best Time of Year to Hike: *Early spring, late fall*

Length: *16.8 miles, round-trip*

Miles to Trailhead from Speedway/Campbell Intersection: *11.1 miles to Visitor Center parking lot*

Directions to Trailhead from Speedway/Campbell Intersection: *Go east on Speedway 5 miles to Wilmot Road. Turn left. Wilmot becomes Tanque Verde at the Pima intersection. Continue on Tanque Verde to Sabino Canyon Road. Turn left and follow the signs to the Sabino Canyon Visitor Center parking lot. It is 0.7 of a mile up the Sabino Canyon Road to the trailhead.*

Esperero Trail begins in Sabino Canyon and climbs 8.4 miles to a 25-foot opening in the crest of a ridge known as the Window. Elevation at the trailhead is 2,850 feet—at the end you'll be at 7,000 feet and be able to see most of Tucson. The trail, originally known as the Dixie Saddle Trail, was constructed in 1924 by Forest Service workers as a trail for use by horseback riders and was described in an early newspaper account as a trail on which "natural wonders meet the gaze at every turn." The reason the name was changed to *Esperero,* Spanish for *hopeful,* is unknown.

Park in the visitor lot at Sabino Canyon and begin walking up the asphalt road into the canyon. At 0.7 of a mile you will see a sign on the left indicating the Cactus picnic area. A few yards past the sign and on the left, another sign indicates Esperero Trail.

The first section of the trail is heavily used, because it is near the Cactus picnic grounds, and several side trails may confuse you. The correct route is level for about 100 yards and then uphill and to the

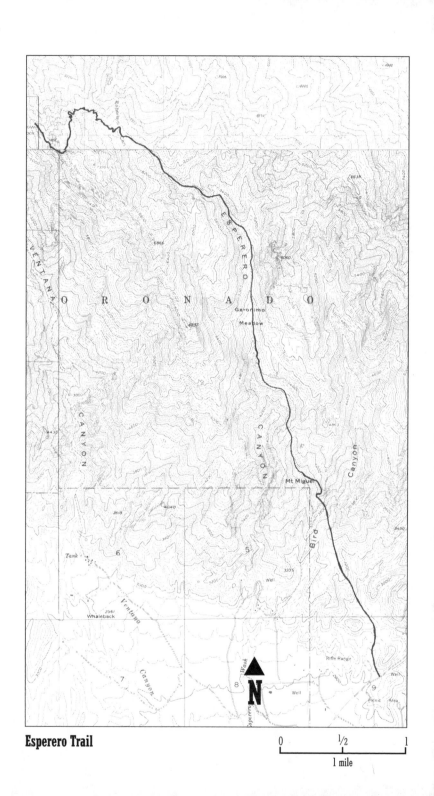

Esperero Trail

0   1/2   1

1 mile

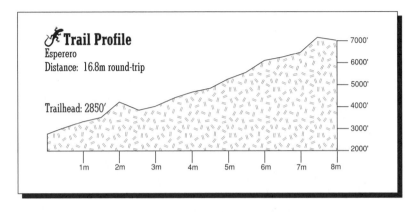

Trail Profile
Esperero
Distance: 16.8m round-trip

Trailhead: 2850'

7000'
6000'
5000'
4000'
3000'
2000'

1m 2m 3m 4m 5m 6m 7m 8m

right. The sign at this junction is frequently vandalized and may be miss-ing when you attempt this hike. At the top of the first hill you reach a signed trail intersection. To the right is a trail that drops into Sabino Canyon. Here, you want to turn left. As you look backward, you realize that you have already gained considerable elevation. From this spot you can see the observatory on Kitt Peak and much of the Tucson valley.

Beyond the intersection, the trail levels and then drops into Rat-tlesnake Canyon. Rattlesnakes deter some people from hiking in the Catalinas. True, Arizona does have more rattlers than any other state in the Union, but, in twenty years of hiking these mountains, I have only seen two. If you see or hear a rattler, stay away from it, and be familiar with proper treatment procedures, which are given in the front of this guide.

The next part of the trail can be confusing. Where there is danger of getting off the trail, low barriers of sticks and stones block the way. Also, cairns mark the trail in critical spots.

After about a mile of strenuous climbing, you level off and then make a sharp descent into Bird Canyon. Here the trail has been rerouted to avoid a short section of private land. As you will note, folks are building homes quite close to the forest boundary.

The vegetation along the trail thus far is typical of the 3,000-foot to 4,000-foot elevation range in the Sonoran Desert—saguaro, barrel, prickly pear, and cholla cacti, ocotillos, mesquite, and palo verde trees, and assorted shrubs, including creosote bush and brittlebush. You may spot deer, javelina, or coyote; and small lizards scatter as you hike. If you are interested in identifying those lizards, the National Forest Visitor

Center in Sabino Canyon has an information sheet that identifies twelve species of lizards. The problem is getting them to hold still long enough for you to identify them!

The trail climbs out of Bird Canyon and then drops into Esperero Canyon. A series of steep step-ups makes this one of the more difficult sections of Esperero, as it hugs the side of the drainage for nearly a mile. It is also one of the prettiest sections, with many large saguaros clinging miraculously to what appears to be barren rock.

Once you come out of the drainage, the real hike begins. It is here that shindaggers make their appearance. Apparently placed here by the "great protector of the Catalinas," this wicked plant has sharp daggers at shin level and attacks anyone who wanders too far off the trail.

This 1/4-mile section of the trail between the drainage and the ridge top has been nicknamed "cardiac gap" by local hikers. Don't let the nickname deter you—it's not *that* bad. A series of switchbacks get you to the top of the ridge. Go slowly and enjoy the view as the city below spreads out across the valley. The flashing tower lights of Tucson Electric Power's substation are easy to spot. Persist, and before you realize it, you are on top of cardiac gap. It takes the average hiker two and one-half to three hours to reach this point, approximately 3 miles.

The ridge is an excellent lunch spot. Turn your back to the city, and the magnificent Catalinas seem to go on forever. Cathedral Rock is the dominant formation of this part of the range. Below, providing there has been enough rainfall, there is a large waterfall where Esperero Canyon empties into the basin. From this point it takes about two hours to return to the Sabino Canyon parking lot. This is a good turnaround point for your first attempt at Esperero Trail.

If you choose to continue, Esperero has a lot more to offer. The trail drops down on the north side of the ridge slightly, climbs steadily for about 1/4 of a mile, and then levels out and circles the basin. Although you are no longer climbing as steeply as before, this section of the trail is still difficult. It is rocky and there are steep step-ups. Since very few people traverse this section, it is usually overgrown and can be tricky to negotiate. Several varieties of oak, juniper, piñon pine, and manzanita grow at this elevation, approximately 5,000 feet. The trail at this point is rugged and overgrown. Not many people make it this far. Congratulate yourself, eat a high-energy bar, and plunge ahead!

Less than a mile from the ridge, the trail passes a large outcropping of rocks on the left and enters Geronimo Meadow. Geronimo

Bridal Veil Falls on the Esperero Trail

Meadow is not a meadow by most definitions. The "meadow" is a level area filled with manzanita and a few pine. There is a good camping spot, complete with a large fire ring and a log to sit on.

Beyond the meadow the trail drops sharply into Esperero Canyon. A creek flows sporadically, mostly in early spring. The trail follows the creek, crisscrossing it several times. If you think you're off the trail, look for cairns. A heavy stand of tall oak trees shades the trail, and this part of the hike is quite pleasant.

One mile upstream, you come to Mormon Spring. A sign indicates a concrete tank off to the right that, in all except the driest season, is filled with water. There are also several pools above the spring that nearly always have water. Don't drink from either source unless you have a way to purify the water.

Beyond Mormon Spring, it's another half-mile to Bridal Veil Falls. The trail is overgrown, difficult to follow, and very steep in places, but the waterfalls at the end make it all worthwhile. About 50 feet tall and surrounded by towering pines, it resembles a bride's veil when sufficient rainfall creates a spray. Even when there has been very little rain, there is usually a trickle, enough for a refreshing shower on a hot afternoon. By the time you reach the waterfall, you will have hiked

5 1/2 miles and gained 2,450 feet in elevation—a respectable day's hike.

Only very well-conditioned, experienced hikers should continue the final 2.9 miles to the Window. In winter the trail could be icy or covered with snow, and the short days may not allow time to return before dark. If you do continue on, expect some major climbing above Bridal Veil Falls and a final sharp descent before you stand in the Window at 7,000 feet. (A shorter route to the Window is via the Ventana Canyon Trail.) In its entirety, Esperero is one of the most difficult trails in the Catalinas. It is also, as you will see in your view from the Window, one of the most rewarding.

Ventana Canyon Trail

General Description: *A challenging hike through one of the most beautiful canyons in the front range of the Catalinas*

Difficulty: *Extremely difficult, some areas of steep climbing*

Best Time of Year to Hike: *Spring, fall*

Length: *12.8 miles, round-trip*

Miles to Trailhead from Speedway/Campbell Intersection: *12.2 miles*

Directions to Trailhead from Speedway/Campbell Intersection: *Go east on Speedway 5 miles to Wilmot Road. Turn left. Wilmot becomes Tanque Verde at the Pima intersection. Continue on Tanque Verde to Sabino Canyon Road. Turn left on Sabino Canyon Road and go 3.7 miles to the intersection of Kolb Road. Turn left on Kolb Road for 3.4 miles, to the entrance to Loew's Ventana Canyon Resort. Turn right 0.1 of a mile until you reach the employees parking lot, which is on the left just before you reach the resort. Park in the spaces reserved for hikers. The trail begins at the northwest corner of the parking lot.*

As you look toward the Catalinas from the Grant-Campbell area, if the light is just right, you can see a tiny hole at the top of the mountain in about the middle of the range. That "tiny" hole is in a large rock fin at the crest of a ridge far above Ventana Canyon and is an oval opening approximately 15 feet high and 25 feet wide, known as the Window, or *Ventana* in Spanish.

It is a challenging 6.4-mile climb up the Ventana Canyon Trail to the Window. Beginning at a 2,950-foot elevation, amid saguaro and mesquite, you eventually reach 7,000 feet, where ponderosa pines tower above you. The nearly 13-mile round-trip will take most of the day.

The newly opened access to Ventana Canyon basically follows the creekbed, climbing in and out several times before reaching the national

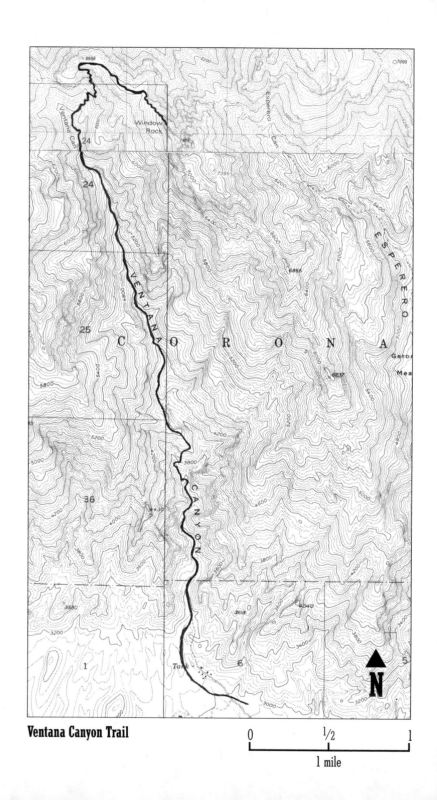

Ventana Canyon Trail

0   1/2   1

1 mile

N

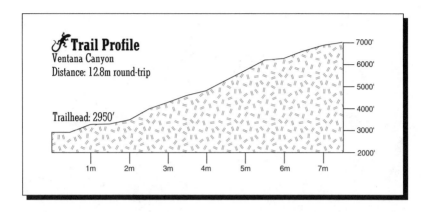

forest boundary. Past the walk-through fence, the steep cliffs of Ventana Canyon rise spectacularly on each side. The trail follows the creek for approximately 1 mile. The creek is dry most of the year, but in late winter and spring it is usually running. After about a mile and a half, you begin to climb out of the bottom of the canyon, up a series of steep switchbacks. There are concrete slabs at intervals across this section of the trail that, although they prevent erosion, make walking more treacherous. This portion of the trail has splendid views of the city below and the Santa Rita Mountains south of Tucson. As you top the first set of switchbacks, you can see part of the golf course of the resort.

You top the hill and circle to the west before dropping down into an area known as Maiden Pools. This is a beautiful section of the canyon with a series of pools, a few large enough for swimming. It is easy to visualize how the area got its name—a beautiful maiden would look right at home here, sunbathing amid the pools and lush vegetation. Flowers and grasses grow in abundance. Large Mexican blue oaks provide shade, and there are many perfect picnic spots. This is a good turnaround point for a half-day hike, because it takes less than two hours to reach this point.

If you plan to continue to the Window, be aware that at Maiden Pools it is very easy to get off the trail, because there are many side trails that lead down to the pools. The trail to the Window stays above the pool area. If you take a side trail, be sure to come back up the same trail you went down and connect with the main trail.

Approach to the Window on the Ventana Canyon Trail

Above Maiden Pools the trail is quite confusing for about a mile. It crosses the creek several times, and some parts are very brushy. Watch carefully for cairns that indicate direction.

About 1 mile past Maiden Pools, you come to a second pool area, smaller than Maiden Pools, but equally pretty. Several large Arizona sycamores, distinguished by the white sections of peeling bark, grow in this area. The canyon here is quite narrow and the pools are below the trail on the canyon floor.

Past the sycamores the climbing begins in earnest. There is a steep section where you gain elevation rapidly, first with a few switchbacks, then continuing nearly straight up. About halfway up this section is a large, smooth rock with two deep bedrock mortars, circular depressions caused by Indian women grinding mesquite beans or other legumes. This is evidence that at one time, nearly 1,000 years ago, Hohokam Indians camped and hunted in this canyon.

A few steps past the mortars look to the right and you will get your first view of the Window. From this vantage point, it looks impossible that you will actually be sitting in the Window in about 2 miles. The steep rock face with the still-tiny-looking opening appears formidable. You can easily see that a fall from the Window would be fatal.

Past the mortars rock, the trail goes through a pretty section. It passes a spring, where there are several small pools of water, and enters a section of ponderosa pine, an indication that you are nearing the highest elevations of the front range of the Catalinas. For a time, you are going directly away from the Window, heading west, and you may question whether you are on the correct trail. Then you make a sharp turn and head directly east toward the Window, switchbacking out of the canyon. About halfway up the switchbacks is a signed trail intersection. From here you can join the Finger Rock Trail and go 2.3 miles east to Mount Kimball. At this intersection, turn right for the final 1.2-mile climb to the Window.

Beyond the sign is a steep, rocky portion of the trail. It crosses the open side of the hill, and here it is very easy to lose your way. Watch carefully for cairns. Since you will want to rest often, fortunately there are excellent views of the valley. As you come to the top of the switchbacks, you have a pleasant surprise. For about 1/2 of a mile the trail crosses a saddle and is level. Your legs by this point really don't know how to walk on level ground. After about 1/4 of a mile on the level area, there is a viewpoint to the left of the trail that provides dramatic views of the other side of the mountain. Biosphere 2 is far off to the right. You can see several new housing developments, and 40 miles north, the triangular outline of Picacho Peak.

The last quarter of a mile climbs steadily to the Window and is a killer, not because it is so terribly steep, but because your legs quickly adjusted to walking on level ground, and, after 6 miles of climbing, you're tired. When you reach the base of a large rock outcropping, you are almost there. Climb carefully over rocks along the base of the cliff and, suddenly, you are looking at the back of the Window.

I cannot emphasize enough the danger of climbing carelessly in the Window. Remember how it looked from the trail? It's at least 100 feet straight down. There is a safe, flat ledge for eating lunch and looking at the views. You can see the University of Arizona, the west side of Tucson, and the downtown area. The A on A Mountain is a tiny letter. Baboquivari Peak is visible, and on a very clear day, you can even see the telescopes at the Kitt Peak Observatory.

After your hike, when you are stopped at the traffic light at Glenn and Campbell headed north, look to your right high up into the Catalinas. If the light is just right, you'll see a tiny opening. Now you know what's really there!

Note: Access through private land was secured by court action. Do not stray from the trail until it crosses the National Forest boundary.

Pontatoc Ridge Trail

General Description: *A short, fun hike to the top of a ridge in the front range of the Catalinas*

Difficulty: *Moderate, short areas of steep climbing*

Best Time of Year to Hike: *Spring, fall, winter*

Length: *5.2 miles, round-trip*

Miles to Trailhead from Speedway/Campbell Intersection: *8.4 miles*

Directions to Trailhead from Speedway/Campbell Intersection: *Go north on Campbell Avenue 6.2 miles to Skyline Drive. Turn right on Skyline Drive for 0.5 of a mile. At this point Skyline divides and turns left. Continue on Skyline for 0.7 of a mile to the intersection of Alvernon Way. Turn left on Alvernon Way, which dead-ends after 1 mile. There is a trailhead parking area on the left. Turn in carefully to avoid the "wrong way" spikes.*

The Pontatoc Ridge Trail is named after the Pontotoc Mine. According to Lutie Wilson, who lives in the renovated cookshack of the mine, her husband Link's uncle, Miles Carpenter, located the mine in 1907. When he located the mine, a group of Indians lived around a nearby spring that had grapevines. The Indians called the area *Pontotoc,* which is a Chickasaw Indian word meaning "hanging grapes." Carpenter and two partners formed the Texas-Arizona Mining Company. Wilson says Carpenter mined three million dollars in copper, silver, and gold from the Pontotoc Mine. Carpenter became prominent in mining circles until his death in 1942. Following his death, his widow Dora sold the Pontotoc Mine to Link and Lutie Wilson. The shafts are fenced, but Lutie still uses water from the mine to water her citrus trees.

On early maps of Tucson, the mine is spelled "Pontotoc," the same as two Chickasaw Indian towns in Mississippi and Oklahoma. By the early 1950s, the spelling had changed to "Pontatoc." This spelling

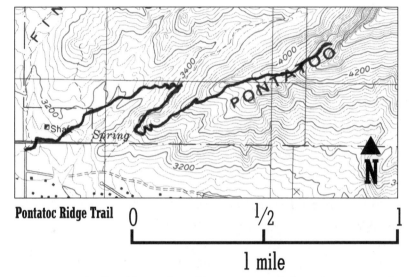

Pontatoc Ridge Trail

0   1/2   1

1 mile

error entered officialdom when the area around the mine was made into the Coronado Foothills Estates in 1961.

For the first 50 yards or so the Pontatoc Trail is part of the Finger Rock Trail. At the top of the first climb, the Pontatoc Trail cuts off to the right. This trail was recently rerouted to skirt new development in the area.

As you begin, look to the northeast. A stark triangular ridge, with what appears to be several caves in the cliff, dominates the skyline. This is Pontatoc Ridge. The Pontatoc Ridge Trail ends to the right of the largest opening in the cliff, which is actually an abandoned mine.

In recent years, the area near the trailhead has become a favorite teenage hangout. There are many side trails leading to fire rings that make the first 0.8-mile of the trail confusing. The following description is purposely detailed. Follow it carefully, and you will be rewarded with a great little hike that provides dramatic views of Tucson. In addition, you'll get a better understanding of the early mining history of the Catalinas.

You may feel like a mouse wandering through a maze in search of cheese on the lower section of this trail! Several false trails lead off to the right and are tempting to take because they appear to head directly for the ridge, but remember to keep bearing slightly to the left, heading for the cliff. The last time I hiked this trail, side trails

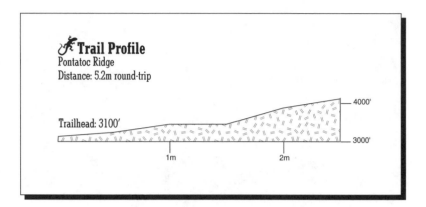

Trail Profile
Pontatoc Ridge
Distance: 5.2m round-trip

Trailhead: 3100'

4000'

3000'

1m   2m

had been blocked off by rows of rocks which, hopefully, have not been disturbed.

After about 0.6 of a mile, the trail drops into a small drainage, comes out, and descends into another somewhat deeper drainage. Shortly you come to a third drainage that is deep and very pronounced. This is the lower part of Pontatoc Canyon. If there has been adequate rainfall, there may be water running. At any time of year there is an assortment of wildflowers that makes this a pretty spot.

It is a steep climb out of the drainage, and you enter an area that is covered with amole (shindaggers), those spear-like plants that attack you at shin level. The vegetation is mostly palo verde and mesquite trees, prickly pear, cholla and barrel cacti, and ocotillos. There is not a very thick stand of saguaros on this trail, unlike most of the trails of the front range.

As you go up the switchbacks, turn right at a signed intersection on the Pontatoc Ridge Trail, which quickly levels off along the side of the ridge. This is a pleasant part of the trail, with excellent views of the west side of Tucson and of Finger Rock. As you round the ridge, the entire city spreads out below.

There is a large, flat, rocky area that is a good spot to have lunch or just relax. If you are careful, this spot is excellent for a hike during a full moon. A perfect scenario is to hike up right before sunset, watch the sun go down, the moon rise, and the lights of the city come on as you enjoy a picnic dinner!

For about 1/2 of a mile the trail is again hard to follow. There are cairns that mark the general direction, but, should they be gone,

Pontatoc Ridge

remember to bear to the left slightly and continue up the ridge. There are several steep step-ups. One section looks like someone deliberately planted teddy bear cholla, and, for about 1/4 of a mile, you have to be very careful not to bump into one, or you will learn why they are called "jumping" cactus.

Beyond the cholla, for about 1/2 of a mile, the trail is a slab of rock, and it is again easy to stray off the trail. There is a large rock outcropping; the best route is to go to the left. Watch carefully for rows of rocks that block the trail. There are times when it appears that you should go to the right, when most of the time the trail is actually to the left. If you do get off the trail, it is not disastrous, and you will wander back on the correct path.

You continue to climb gradually for about 3/4 of a mile, occasionally encountering a few minor switchbacks, including one set that goes to the right. The views as you crest the ridge are spectacular. Below, you can see where the Pontatoc Canyon Trail switchbacks out of the canyon.

From this point the Pontatoc Ridge Trail is distinct, as it makes its way to the mine area. Very shortly you come to a saddle. To the right of the trail are excellent views of the east side of Tucson. You look down on the Skyline Country Club and the homes of the Skyline Country Club Estates.

Past the saddle the trail becomes steeper and is quite rocky. As you get closer to the ridge, there is more evidence of mining activity, and the openings in the cliff are clearly visible. A sign indicates the end of the Pontatoc Ridge Trail. It is dangerous to proceed beyond this point.

Finger Rock Trail

General Description: *A steep climb through a beautiful canyon with spectacular views*

Difficulty: *Extremely difficult, steep, continuous climbing after the first mile*

Best Time of Year to Hike: *Spring and fall*

Length: *10 miles, round-trip*

Miles to Trailhead from Speedway/Campbell Intersection: *8.4 miles*

Directions to Trailhead from Speedway/Campbell Intersection: *Go north on Campbell Avenue 6.2 miles to Skyline Drive. Turn right on Skyline Drive for 0.5 of a mile. At this point Skyline divides and turns left. Continue on Skyline for 0.7 of a mile to the intersection of Alvernon Way. Turn left on Alvernon Way, which dead-ends. A trailhead parking area is on the left. Turn in carefully, avoiding the "wrong way" spikes.*

A dominant landmark of the Catalinas is Finger Rock, a tall rock spire that points skyward about midway through the range. It is possible to get a better view of that rock spire by climbing the Finger Rock Trail to Mount Kimball, through some of the most spectacular scenery in the Catalinas.

The well-marked trail begins to the right of a sign at the end of the street. After an initial short climb, the trail is basically level for 1.1 miles. The trail heads into Finger Rock Canyon, through an impressive stand of saguaros. The spring, usually a permanent water source, empties into a partially covered concrete tank to the left of the trail. Do not follow the trail that continues level beyond the spring, unless you want to spend some time in the canyon bottom.

The Finger Rock Trail switchbacks to the right, up the side of the canyon. As you work your way up the switchbacks, Finger Rock

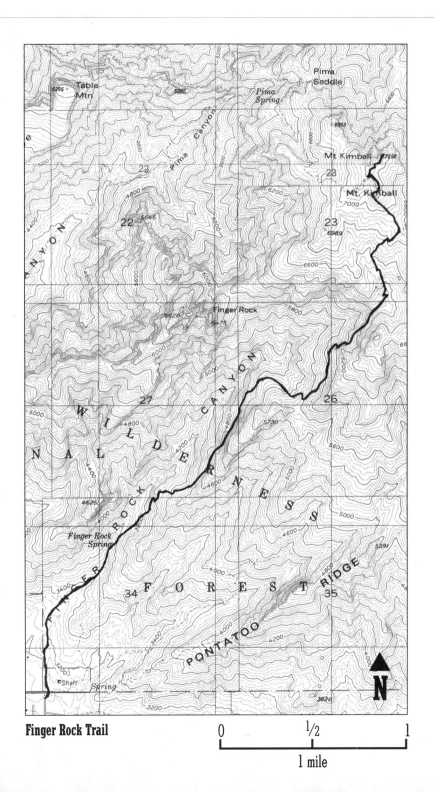

Finger Rock Trail

0   1/2   1

1 mile

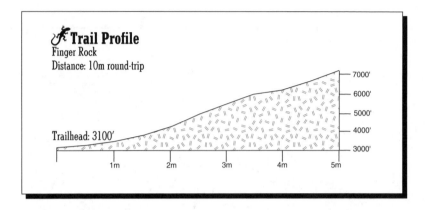

🦎 **Trail Profile**
Finger Rock
Distance: 10m round-trip

7000'
6000'
5000'
4000'
3000'

Trailhead: 3100'

1m   2m   3m   4m   5m

appears larger; however, this is as close as the trail comes to the actual rock formation. This initial climb up the switchbacks is one of the hardest parts of the trail, with steep step-ups and several areas of loose rock.

After the switchbacks, the trail drops into a small drainage. This section has many amoles and it is important to stay on the trail to avoid being punctured in the shins by the sharp spines of the plant. The trail continues to climb around the canyon basin. There are no parts of the Finger Rock Trail that could be called easy. In fact, except for a few very short sections, the Finger Rock Trail is relentless in its climb to Mount Kimball. The views are excellent, however, and always worth the climb.

After about 2 miles you reach a large, flat rock on the left, overlooking the canyon. You have gained enough elevation that the saguaros have disappeared and have been replaced by piñon pine, juniper, and several varieties of oak. Finger Rock is now obscured by the cliffs and will not be visible for the remainder of the hike.

There are some places in this portion of the trail that can be confusing. There is a side trail, called Linda Vista Saddle, to the right that leads to an overlook of the city, but it involves some very steep, unnecessary climbing. Wait a few hundred yards for a second trail to the right that will get you to the saddle with very little effort.

Before reaching this second trail to the right, you will see a distinct trail to the left. Even though this trail is blocked by a row of small rocks, it looks like the logical trail to take to Mount Kimball, and many hikers mistakenly head in this direction. Don't! Continue on the main

Hiker studies saguaro on the Finger Rock Trail

trail, which bears to the right. On this main trail, and immediately after a short steep section, a spur trail goes to the right and is the correct route to reach Linda Vista Saddle. The spur trail is level except for a brief climb at the end.

Linda Vista means beautiful view, and that's exactly what the area provides. From the saddle, you can see the entire Tucson valley. Westin La Paloma Resort looks like a pink dollhouse below. This is a good turnaround spot if you want a short hike. It takes about two and a half hours to hike the 3 miles to the saddle.

If you choose to continue the remaining 2 miles to Mount Kimball, expect some steep climbing ahead. Take the spur trail from Linda Vista Saddle back to the main trail and continue around the basin. Several varieties of oak shade the trail, and you pass beneath huge boulders. Mistletoe hangs from most of the trees. For a short period the trail is smooth, but it soon becomes rocky again. Baboquivari Peak, Kitt Peak, and most of the west side of the city, including downtown Tucson and the white buildings of the Arizona Health Sciences Center, are visible from here.

The scenery in this section is dramatic, with stark cliffs towering above the tall pines. The carpet of soft pine needles is quite a treat after the rocky trail. There are several excellent camping spots and two small drainages that are likely to have water during winter and early spring.

Past the pines, you come to a more open area, covered with manzanitas and small oaks. The city spreads out below and the views are great, but, unfortunately, pine needles yield to rocks again.

As you begin to top out, you come to a small saddle and a directional sign. Turn left on the Pima Canyon Trail, Number 62. Past the sign the trail turns north and once again begins to climb through piñon pine and juniper. Soon you are again hiking under tall pines, and this is a lovely portion of the hike.

Follow the trail along the crest to the right for about 200 yards, and you will come to a large, flat rock outcropping that is an excellent lunch spot and lookout. Depending on your conditioning, it will take four to five hours to reach Mount Kimball and almost as long to return.

To use an old hiking cliché, the views are worth every step. The Finger Rock Trail takes you to the heart of the Catalinas. Cathedral Rock and Mount Lemmon are to the east. You can see part of Pusch Ridge to the west; Picacho Peak and Sun City Tucson are to the northwest; and, almost due north, you can see the white structures of Biosphere II.

Most who hike to the summit of Mount Kimball would be surprised to learn that the peak was named for an early developer—Frederick E. A. Kimball. Kimball moved to Tucson in 1899 and lived here until his death in 1930. He was one of the first property owners in Summerhaven and, during the summers, served as postmaster of the tiny village. He urged the building of a short road to Mount Lemmon and promoted the development of Summerhaven as a summer recreation area. At the time of his death, Kimball was secretary-treasurer of the Summerhaven Land and Improvement Company.

In addition to his interest in Summerhaven, Kimball owned a printing business and a book and stationery store in Tucson. At one time he was a reporter for the *Arizona Daily Star.* He served four terms in the Arizona legislature and, at the time of his death, was in the state senate. As senator, Kimball secured passage of the state's first child welfare bill and supported the establishment of the Catalina Game Preserve.

An ardent outdoorsman, Kimball was a member of the Game Protective Association and an organizer of the Tucson Natural History Society. It was this group that appealed to the United States Geographic Board (USGB) for the naming of a peak in the Catalinas in his memory. The previously unnamed peak was officially designated as Mount Kimball by the USGB on February 4, 1931.

Although Kimball spent much time hiking in the Catalinas in the area around Summerhaven, it is not known whether he ever stood atop the peak that was named after him. It is certain that he would have been pleased with the choice.

Pima Canyon Trail

General Description: *A long hike through a beautiful canyon into one of the most rugged areas of the Catalina Mountains*

Difficulty: *Extremely difficult, easy for first 3.2 miles*

Best Time of Year to Hike: *Early spring, late fall*

Length: *14.2 miles, round-trip*

Miles to Trailhead from Speedway/Campbell Intersection: *10 miles*

Directions to Trailhead from Speedway/Campbell Intersection: *Go north on Campbell for 5.4 miles to Skyline Drive. Turn left on Skyline and continue to Ina Road. Continue on Ina until you reach Christie Drive. Follow Christie Drive north until it dead-ends at Magee Road. Turn right on Magee, and you will see the Iris O. Dewhirst Trailhead parking area straight ahead and on the right.*

The Pima Canyon Trail is one of the most popular trails in the front range of the Catalinas. It is easily accessible, not too difficult for the first 3 miles, and beautiful. Beginning in 1996, the U.S. Forest Service instituted new regulations to protect the dwindling bighorn sheep herd believed to inhabit the upper reaches of Pima Canyon. From January through April, the new regulations include restricting any off-trail hiking or camping beyond 400 feet of authorized trails and limiting day hiking groups to fifteen and overnight parties to six. Dogs are forbidden on any part of the trail.

The trail leaves from the east corner of the trailhead parking lot, past a plaque placed on a boulder in memory of Tom Bingham. Bingham loved hiking the Pima Canyon Trail and was instrumental in securing unrestricted public access to the trail, which crosses private property before entering the national forest. Bingham fell to his death on April 12, 1992, while rock climbing by himself in Pima Canyon.

Past the plaque interpretive signs introduce hikers to Pima Canyon. The first 0.75 mile crosses private land through a fenced corridor before

Pima Canyon Trail

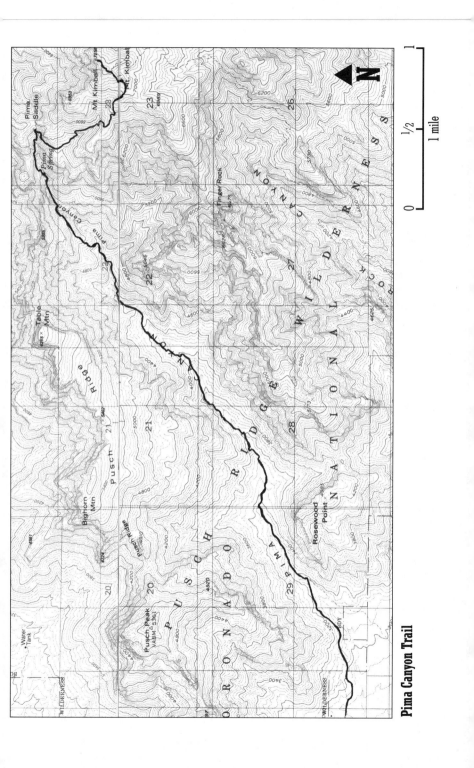

N

0   ½   1

1 mile

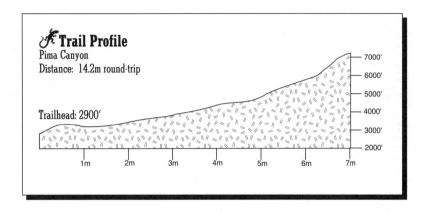

Trail Profile
Pima Canyon
Distance: 14.2m round-trip

Trailhead: 2900'

entering the National Forest and climbing to the base of the mountains. The vegetation is typical of the 2,500- to 3,200-foot elevations of the Sonoran Desert—saguaro, prickly pear, barrel, and cholla cacti, catclaw, ocotillo, brittlebush, mesquite, and palo verde. The views of Tucson from this section show the entire valley. South, the 9,453-foot peak of Mount Wrightson is clearly visible, as is the A on A Mountain. Far to the west, Baboquivari Peak, sacred mountain of the Tohono O'odham Indians, and the Kitt Peak National Observatory are the dominant landmarks.

After about a mile of easy hiking with some brief climbing, the trail drops sharply into the creek bed. The creek is dry much of the year, but is lovely when it is flowing, mostly in winter and spring.

As you cross the creek and round a curve, the city disappears. This is one of the joys of living in Tucson and having the Catalinas in your backyard. Within an hour of hiking, you can escape the city. The trail parallels the stream for the next 2 miles, occasionally crossing to the other side. Even when the stream is running, it is easy to boulder-hop across. One-half of a mile into the canyon, the first cottonwoods appear. Soon the giant trees provide a canopy, and you are walking in the shade. This is one of the prettiest areas on the lower portion of the Pima Canyon Trail.

As you leave the dense trees, the canyon opens up. The drainage from Pusch Ridge comes in from the north. Pusch Ridge is the prime habitat of the bighorn sheep, and, if you're lucky, you may spot one of these magnificent creatures standing on a rock outcropping.

Here the trail becomes confusing, crossing the narrow stream bed several times. If you are in doubt as to the correct route of the trail,

Hikers on the Pima Canyon Trail

stop, look for cairns indicating direction, or rows of rocks blocking the wrong way. The ascent into the canyon becomes slightly more difficult. After a particularly steep, but mercifully short, climb, you'll know you are nearing the Pima Canyon Dam. You will cross several large slabs of rock right before the dam.

The Pima Canyon Dam was built by the Arizona Game and Fish Division as a source of water for wildlife. This is a good lunch spot. Secluded in a bend of the canyon, you would never know that a city of seven hundred thousand people was only 3 miles away. Flowers cling to the drainage around the dam. Birds chatter and occasionally dive down for a drink. It is no wonder that in an earlier time, around A.D. 1000, this spot was home to the Hohokam Indians. Two hundred yards to the left of the dam as you face down the canyon are bedrock mortars, depressions in the rock formed by Indian women grinding mesquite beans. Two mortars are very deep, and there are several smaller ones nearby. It is easy to imagine Indian women sitting on the rocks, chatting, and grinding beans, while their men hunted.

It takes the average hiker about two hours to reach this point. You have hiked 3 miles and gained 800 feet in elevation, from 2,900 feet at the trailhead to 3,700 feet at the dam. The dam is a short side-trip; the trail continues across a rock slab and away from the dam. This first portion of the trail is an excellent introduction to the canyons of the Catalinas and is a good turnaround spot for a beginning hiker.

A lot more is ahead if you choose to continue up the canyon. For another mile the elevation gain is gradual. The saguaros disappear and are replaced by Mexican blue oaks. The trail crosses one of the loveliest spots in Pima Canyon. For about a mile the trail is high above the creek. A bit farther and you cross large slabs of rock, interspersed with pools of water. To the right is a dam, this one larger than the first. Beyond this dam, the trail begins to climb sharply. You are headed into one of the most rugged sections of the Catalinas and one of the most dramatically beautiful.

You climb continually for another mile until you reach Pima Canyon Spring. At the spring you will have come 5.2 miles from the trailhead and gained 2,550 feet in elevation. This spring provides a permanent source of water. As you approach the spring there are two concrete tanks, which, as you will see shortly, are connected by pipe to a spring above. There are several good campsites around the spring area.

Above the spring you have to be a serious, well-conditioned hiker to continue. Study the map carefully to get an indication of what is ahead. Mount Kimball is at 7,200 feet, you are at 5,550 feet. It is a rough 1.9-mile climb to the summit.

As you leave the canyon from the spring, you climb sharply along an open hillside. The views of the city to the south and of the canyon to the north are awesome. As you're looking up the canyon, actually climbing it doesn't seem possible.

A half-mile into the climb, you come to a small sign pointing to Pima Saddle. A short spur trail leads to the saddle, and if you have time, the views are worth it. You get a glimpse of the "other side of the mountain." Between this sign and Mount Kimball is some of the most difficult climbing and trail finding in the Catalinas. As my hiking companion said, "There are one hundred places you can break your leg," and, a few minutes later, I heard, "This is the worst trail I have ever been on!" The trail bears to the right around a large rock outcropping. Although there are numerous cairns that lead straight up the drainage, the trail goes to the right, and shortly becomes more defined.

Despite the difficulty, in terms of scenery and views the trip up the canyon and to Mount Kimball is, for want of a better word, spectacular.

How many people can say they have seen the back of Finger Rock? As you near Mount Kimball, the ponderosa pines tower above you. You feel like you are on top of the world. Look north, and you see Biosphere II near Oracle, to the east is Mount Lemmon, look south, and all of Tucson spreads out below.

The trip up and down the Pima Canyon Trail requires the entire day. Depending on your conditioning, I would estimate at least six hours up and five hours back, allowing reasonable time for resting and enjoying the views from the top. An interesting variation is to come up the Pima Canyon Trail and descend by way of the shorter Finger Rock Trail. This requires leaving a vehicle at each trailhead, but will shorten the return trip.

Romero Canyon Trail

General Description: *A hike to a canyon with deep year-round pools suitable for swimming*

Difficulty: *Moderate, some areas of steep climbing*

Best Time of Year to Hike: *Spring, fall, winter*

Length: *5.6 miles, round-trip*

Miles to Trailhead from Speedway/Campbell Intersection: *15.7 miles*

Directions to Trailhead from Speedway/Campbell Intersection: *Go north on Campbell Avenue 6.2 miles to Skyline Drive. Turn left on Skyline Drive and take it to Oracle Road. Turn right on Oracle and continue north to the entrance of Catalina State Park. There is a $3 per-vehicle charge to enter the park. Drive to the trailhead parking area at the end of the road. The Romero Canyon Trailhead is to the right, past the bulletin board and rest rooms.*

Romero Canyon is a spectacular canyon on the north side of the Santa Catalina Mountains. The Romero Canyon Trail leads into the mountains and connects with the West Fork of Sabino Trail, enabling the adventurous hiker to cross the mountains into Sabino Canyon, or, by intersecting with the Mount Lemmon Trail, to climb to the summit of Mount Lemmon. This trail description is for the first 2.8 miles of the Romero Canyon Trail, the portion that leads to an area known as Romero Pools.

The pools and canyon are named after Fabian Romero, who, in 1889, established Rancho Romero in Canada del Oro, near where Oracle Junction is today. The ranch, the first in that area, covered 4,800 acres.

The trail into this lush canyon leaves across from the parking lot and immediately crosses Canada del Oro Wash. If there has been adequate rainfall or snowmelt, the wash is running, and you must boulder-hop or wade across. Once across the wash, the trail climbs

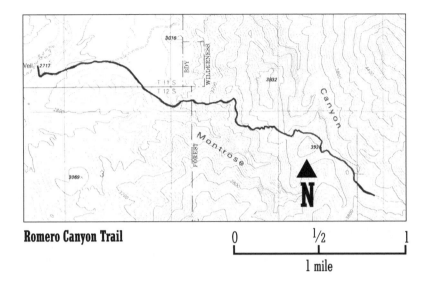

Romero Canyon Trail

0   ¹/₂   1

1 mile

immediately to the east. A newly constructed wide sandy path climbs the hill. At the top of the first rise is a level area where two benches provide a good spot to sit, rest, and view the riparian area below.

The trail continues southeast to the intersection of the Canyon Loop Trail and the Romero Canyon Trail. The Canyon Loop Trail is a pleasant 2 1/2-mile loop trail that connects with the Sutherland Trail to return to the parking area. The Romero Canyon Trail continues straight ahead and is level and sandy and wide enough to be a road. It passes through a large stand of mesquite and heads directly for the base of the mountains. After 1/4 of a mile, another intersection is reached, that of Romero and Montrose Canyons. Montrose Canyon is a deep canyon to the west with several large pools. A steep trail leads down into the canyon. The trail is not maintained and a sign warns, "Danger—Unsafe Footing Beyond this Point."

The Romero Canyon Trail climbs to the left of the intersection and immediately becomes narrow and rocky. At the National Forest Boundary sign, hikers are warned that dogs are not permitted beyond this point. The trail climbs steadily, and the views of both the valley and the mountains are excellent. This is a heavily used trail, and many

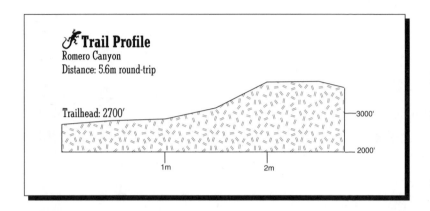

hikers have made side trails leading to lookout points, which may temporarily cause you to stray off the trail. Also, the trail occasionally splits, but always returns to the main trail, making whichever direction you take all right. For the most part the trail is clearly marked, and there is no question as to the route.

The trail circles the drainage, gradually climbing toward the crest of the ridge. The vegetation is diverse in the shelter of the drainage. Small saguaros are thriving under their "nurse" trees. In spring the wildflowers are profuse. The entire area is a jumble of boulders.

As the trail continues to climb, it goes through a slit in the rock and then seriously begins climbing toward the crest of a ridge. A series of steep, rocky switchbacks brings you to the top of the ridge. There are several places where the trail has been *shortcut,* a hiking term that means that hikers have cut across a switchback, going straight up the trail rather than using the switchback. Shortcutting causes erosion and is not good hiking etiquette. Unfortunately, any trail that is used by a great number of people attracts many who are not concerned about the effects of their actions on the environment. In a few years this section of the trail will be badly eroded unless preventive maintenance is done.

The views of the Catalinas from the ridge are spectacular in this area, and you realize you are entering rugged country. From the crest of this first ridge, the trail descends briefly and crosses a saddle between two ridges. To the left, after about 0.2 of a mile, you get your first view of Romero Canyon. There is a large waterfall at the base of the canyon. It appears as if it is possible to climb down to the waterfall

Romero Pools

from this point, but the route is treacherous, and it is better to work your way down farther along the trail and nearer the creek.

Fortunately the trail does not climb the steep ridge in front of you but circles it to the northeast. This portion of the trail, shaded by tall oak trees, is especially beautiful, with the views of the canyon on the left. As the trail drops into Romero Canyon, you can see the area called Romero Pools. It takes the average hiker two to two and a half hours to reach the pool area. The trail crosses the stream, and from there it is possible to boulder-hop to the several pools that continue downstream. Less than 0.25 of a mile upstream you'll find another series of pools.

The pools are deep and, on hot days, invite swimmers. I am always amazed at the impact of water in the desert. Sitting in the shade of a tall juniper tree, dangling your feet in the cool water, and watching blue jays dart between the trees, it is hard to believe you're in the heart of the Sonoran Desert.

Prison Camp to Sabino Canyon Trail

General Description: *An easy walk, mostly downhill, from an old prison camp to Sabino Canyon*

Difficulty: *Moderate, few areas with steep switchbacks*

Best Time of Year to Hike: *Winter, early spring, late fall*

Length: *7.6 miles one way*

Miles to Trailhead from Speedway/Campbell Intersection: *20.4 miles*

Directions to Trailhead from Speedway/Campbell Intersection: *This hike requires two vehicles. The ideal way to do it is to leave a car at the Sabino Canyon Visitor Center and have someone drive you to the Prison Camp Road. Drive east on Speedway Boulevard to the intersection of Wilmot Road. Turn left on Wilmot. Wilmot Road becomes Tanque Verde Road at the intersection of Pima and Wilmot. Continue on Tanque Verde Road to Sabino Canyon Road. Turn left on Sabino Canyon Road and leave one vehicle at the Sabino Canyon Visitor Center parking lot. Retrace your route on Sabino Canyon Road to Tanque Verde. Turn left on Tanque Verde Road to the Catalina Highway. Turn left on Catalina Highway and drive 0.4 of a mile past Milepost 7, where an intersection sign indicates a paved road to the left. Turn in this road and drive 200 yards to a paved parking area on the right. This is the site of the old prison camp and the starting point of the hike.*

If you want to be somewhat poetic, tell friends you are hiking from the dam to the tram! We'll leave the parking lot of an old prison camp, hike to Sycamore Dam, and end up at stop 9 of the Sabino Canyon Tram, where $6 will get us a ride to our waiting car.

Only the foundations remain of what was once a large prison camp. The camp resulted from efforts of *Tucson Citizen* editor Frank

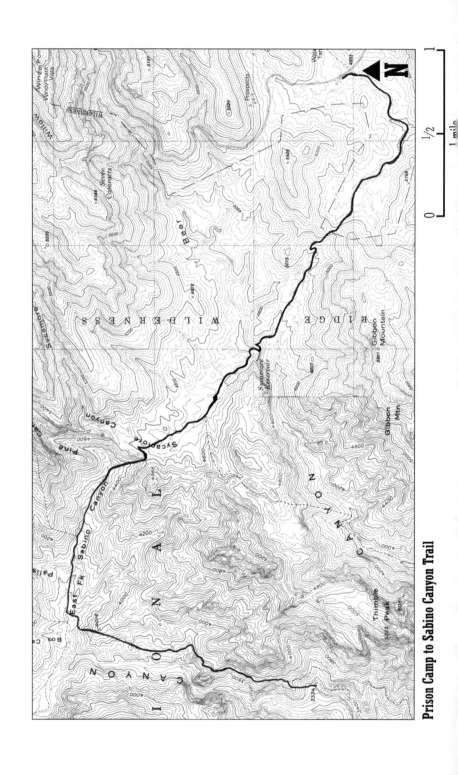

Prison Camp to Sabino Canyon Trail

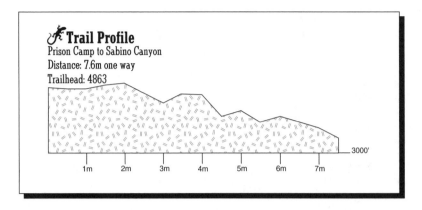

⚲ Trail Profile
Prison Camp to Sabino Canyon
Distance: 7.6m one way
Trailhead: 4863

3000'

1m 2m 3m 4m 5m 6m 7m

Harris Hitchcock, who, in the early 1930s, tried to get a road built to
Mount Lemmon. When two bond issues failed, General Hitchcock, as
he was known from his term as Postmaster General of the United
States, convinced an old Washington friend, Stanford Bates, director
of the Federal Bureau of Prisons, to supply prison labor for construction of the road, thus transferring funding for the project to the federal government.

Construction began on a permanent camp to house the prisoners
at Vail Corral Basin, near today's Molino Basin Campground. When
finally completed in February 1939, the camp had a total of fifty-five
buildings, including barracks, a kitchen, mess hall, a power and steam
heating plant, laundry, training shop, garage, and housing for officers
and guards.

The General Hitchcock Highway, as it was officially named, received final inspection on February 28, 1951. Prison records show
that 8,003 inmates were assigned to the Tucson Prison Camp during
road construction. The 25 miles of road cost an average of $4,000 per
mile. The prison camp remained open until 1967, when the Bureau
of Prisons closed the camp because of the high cost of operation. In
1973 the Forest Service razed the abandoned prison camp buildings.

The site of the prison camp is now the Gordon Hirabayashi Recreation Site, named in honor of a Japanese-American interred here during World War II. Walk through the gate to the end of the campground.
A small trail sign on the left indicates Sycamore Reservoir Trail #39.
Follow the directional arrow to the top of the hill where another trail
sign indicates that the Sycamore Reservoir Trail #39 turns to the right.

After a brief downhill stretch, the trail, which is part of the official Arizona Trail, begins to climb into a saddle, where a large sign depicts the route of the Arizona Trail. Now closed to vehicles, the road on the right was the supply road to the Sycamore Reservoir. Our route is to follow the Sycamore Reservoir Trail Number 39. It is a mile from this sign to the dam.

As you begin switchbacking down the trail, look on the left for several pillars of varying heights, the tallest being about 5 feet. These were the supports that carried the pipeline that brought utility water from the reservoir to the prison camp. As you near the dam, the trail veers right and for a short time joins the road that led to the dam. A path goes off to the right at the bottom of the hill. This will be our eventual route, but for now continue straight ahead and take a look at the dam. You pass a concrete slab that once held the pumphouse for the dam.

When the prison camp was in operation, this dam backed up a large reservoir. Even today it is a massive structure and water usually roars over the spillway. When you tire of looking at the dam, it's time to head for the tram. This part of the trail can be confusing, so follow the directions carefully. You are headed for Sycamore Canyon, the *first* canyon to the right as you look down the spillway of the dam. To get to the trail, you must make a loop to avoid the water and dense vegetation near the dam.

Leave the platform and follow the path back in the direction of the trail. The path veers to the left and follows the base of a hill for about 100 yards before turning sharply to the left and crossing into Sycamore Canyon.

This is where you may get confused, depending on whether water has recently obliterated the path. Make the left turn just before a large rock protruding from the sand. Follow the path across the sandy drainage, crossing the water, if there is any running, and begin to climb out of the drainage on what is now a definite trail and shortly becomes part of the old road. If you stray too far before turning left, you will quickly realize that you are getting too far away from Sycamore Canyon. If this happens, turn back and work your way to the trail.

After crossing the creek, the trail becomes distinct and begins to climb gradually. For about 1/2 of a mile the trail follows the creek bed and is rocky. Watch carefully for when the trail leaves the rocks, leaves the creek bed, and bears to the right. As it does, the trail begins to climb more steeply, goes through a thick stand of manzanitas, and

Prison Camp to Sabino Canyon Trail, Sycamore Dam

becomes more open. In summer, this portion of the trail is deadly, but in winter, it is a perfect hike. The trail drops and crosses the stream. The trail climbs out of the creek, winds to the left, and begins to climb to a saddle. Right before the saddle, the Bear Canyon Trail Number 29 turns to the left. Sycamore Reservoir Trail Number 39 ends at this intersection, and we now join East Fork Trail Number 24A, which bears to the right and leads into Sabino Basin.

The East Fork Trail switchbacks sharply down toward Sabino Basin and is a spectacular section of trail. Across the canyon, you see the switchbacks of the Palisades Trail as it comes down from the Palisades Ranger Station. There are some steep drop-offs, and you have to watch for loose rocks, but for the most part, this is a well-marked and maintained trail. As the trail reaches Sabino Creek, a sign indicates the intersection of the Palisades and East Fork Trails. We continue on the East Fork Trail, paralleling the stream for much of the way. The trail comes out into the open before circling back and rejoining the creek bed. A sign indicates Box Camp Trail, which comes down from Milepost 22 on the General Hitchcock Highway.

You quickly come to a major trail intersection having several signs to direct the hiker. Since you are headed for the tram, your route should cross the creek and follow Sabino Canyon Trail Number 23 for 2.5 miles out of the basin. It quickly switchbacks away from the creek and offers great views of the basin and the Catalina Mountains. As you top the final ridge, you can see the road and usually the tram approaching. Partway down the final switchbacks, Phoneline Trail Number 27 cuts off to the left. If you are feeling particularly ambitious, you can follow this trail out of the canyon. Should you opt for the tram, give the driver $6, climb on board, and relax.

Butterfly Trail

see note page 156*

General Description: *A beautiful high-elevation hike through thick pine forests and past a permanent spring*

Difficulty: *Moderate*

Best Time of Year to Hike: *Summer, spring, fall*

Length: *5.7 miles from Soldier Camp to Palisades Ranger Station*

Miles to Trailhead from Speedway/Campbell Intersection: *33.8 miles*

Directions to Trailhead from Speedway/Campbell Intersection: *This hike is best done using a two-car shuttle. Drive east on Speedway Boulevard to Wilmot Road. Turn left on Wilmot Road. Wilmot Road turns into Tanque Verde Road at Pima. Continue on Tanque Verde Road to the Catalina Highway. Turn left on Catalina Highway to Mount Lemmon. Follow the Catalina Highway up the mountain to the Palisades Ranger Station. Leave one car at the Ranger Station and drive 2.9 miles farther to a signed and paved parking area on the right near Soldier Camp Road. The Butterfly Trail trailhead is at this parking area.*

On July 25, 1935, 1,000 acres were set aside near Butterfly Peak to preserve one of the most varied areas of vegetation in the southwest. Ranging in elevation from 8,300 feet near Kellogg Mountain to 6,700 feet at Novio Spring, the Butterfly Trail is a classroom for the botanist and hiker.

The Butterfly Trail begins as an old jeep road. After 200 yards the road forks. Take the fork to the left. The road dead-ends and becomes a trail. The correct trail is on the left side of the end of the road.

The trail begins as a long, gradual slope down the north side of the ridge through thick forests of ponderosa pine and fir. Through the trees you can catch a glimpse of the large mine complex at San Manuel, including two smokestacks and a large tailings pond.

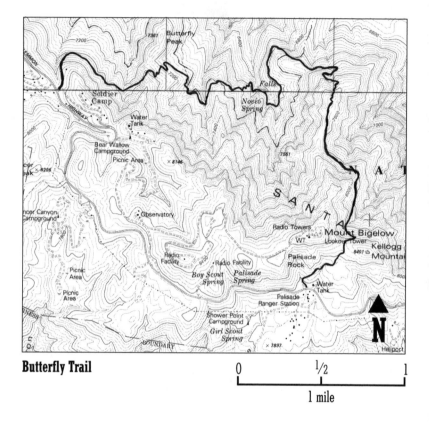

Butterfly Trail

0                    $1/2$ 1

1 mile

The trail circles the basin to the point of a ridge, where a rocky outcropping makes a good stopping spot. From this outcropping the trail turns to the right and switchbacks steeply down the mountain. After about a mile a faint trail leads to Butterfly Peak, 0.4 of a mile ahead. The Butterfly Trail continues to switchback to the right and quickly comes to an open area with few trees. The hillside here is covered with large ferns. You soon return to the magnificent huge ponderosa pines. The cool shade and green vegetation is welcome in summer, when Tucson temperatures are normally at least 100 degrees.

At 1.4 miles there is a signed trail intersection. Continue straight ahead. There is a slight uphill trek before the trail levels off and drops into a ravine. Water is trickling in this ravine for most of the year. These ravines are beautiful areas. Usually devoid of trees, they are covered

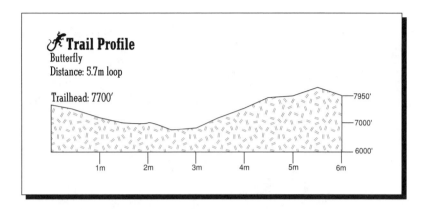

🦎 **Trail Profile**
Butterfly
Distance: 5.7m loop

Trailhead: 7700'

with flowers. In early summer, butterflies hover around the plants, probably the original reason for the name of the peak and the trail. After climbing out of the ravine, the trail winds along the side of the hill for a quarter of a mile, before dropping into another larger ravine.

After climbing out of this ravine, the trail again goes around the hill, through pine and fir. After a quarter of a mile, the trail again begins to switchback steeply down the hill and becomes rocky for a time. It soon emerges onto an open ridge. The television towers are visible to the southwest. Views of the mine from this point are excellent. You are looking down into Alder Canyon. The switchbacks leading down into the canyon are very steep. The east side of the canyon is exposed, with the vegetation being mostly scrub oak. As you approach the bottom, the trees reappear, this time pines and some large alders and oaks.

As you drop down into the head of the canyon, there is a huge boulder on the right. From this point on, most of your route will be uphill until a slight down grade into the Palisades Ranger Station. About 50 yards past the huge rock, you begin to see large shelves of rock on the left. At the base of the rocks are small pools of water. If the runoff is enough, there will be a falls in this area. This area is known as Novio Spring. The trail goes along the creek through a spectacular section. There are large ferns, flowers, and small pools of water. Butterflies and hummingbirds flitter about the flowers.

Immediately after the trail turns left and crosses the last fork of the creek before starting uphill, a faint trail leads to the right to the wreckage site of an F-86 Sabrejet. On July 8, 1957, two pilots from Davis

Butterfly Trail

Monthan Air Force Base were on a routine training flight when their jets collided. With amazing presence of mind, both pilots ejected safely. One of the jets came down near an access road and was hauled away. Parts of the second jet are still here, too heavy and in too remote an area to carry out. After viewing the wreckage, return to the main trail and begin the climb out.

The trail switchbacks steeply out of the canyon and away from the creek. One of the most interesting things about this trail is the changing vegetation. About 1/2 of a mile past the creek there is an area of really mixed vegetation. This is at about 6,000 feet elevation. There are fir, ponderosa pine, oak, and locust trees. It is like nature wasn't exactly sure what belonged here—or conditions are right for a variety of trees. As the trail climbs the side of the hill, it comes to an open section with mostly scrub oak. The views of Alder Canyon are good, and you can appreciate the vastness of the area you are hiking.

There are quite a few yucca plants, Russian thistle, and even prickly pear and hedgehog cacti. Alligator juniper begins to appear. You quickly come to a saddle, which is a little over halfway into the hike. From here the trailhead at Soldier Camp is 3.2 miles. Palisades Ranger Station is 2.5 miles away. Continue ahead across the saddle and slightly to the right.

The trail again changes character and becomes very pleasant and cool. The mine and other side of the mountain are once again in view. From the saddle, the trail climbs gradually through a thick pine and fir forest. A small stand of aspen is trying to survive in the midst of the forest; some are huge trees and others are very small and will probably be choked out. It is an incredibly beautiful area.

The trail climbs out of this section into a small saddle. A trail leads off to the left to several good campsites. The Butterfly Trail continues to the right, switchbacking briefly to a rock outcropping with a seat carved out especially for you—or so it seems. From this seat, the San Pedro River is visible as a line of green.

Past this rock the trail levels off and goes around the ridge, through scrub oak. It passes a large outcropping of rock on the right. There are several nice camp spots along this section, as evidenced by the fire rings. Past the level section, the trail climbs gradually along the steep side of the hill. A fall would lead to a long tumble. There are a few open areas, but for the most part, from here to the end of the trail you will be hiking in shade. You are now very close to the radio towers. One

you will be hiking in shade. You are now very close to the radio towers. One appears to be about 1/2 of a mile above you as you cross an open area across a slab of rocks.

Past this slab of rocks, the trail climbs steeply for 200 yards and reenters a thickly forested area, mostly fir and some oak. The trail in this section climbs gradually. It is smooth and covered with fir needles. It is so thick that the sunlight barely filters through. This is one of the prettiest sections of the trail. Basically the trail is a steep but gradual climb, with a few areas of very steep climbing. As the trail approaches the saddle, there are some huge fir trees near the top. As you come to the saddle, you are only 0.5 of a mile from the Palisades Ranger Station. The last half-mile is downhill through ponderosa pine is an open park-like area covered with ferns. You catch glimpses of Tucson and understand why our southern Arizona mountain ranges are often called islands in the sky.

As of this printing, the Butterfly Trail is closed as a result of the summer of 2002 Bullock Fire. The Butterfly Trail will be re-opened as soon as the area is safe to enter. To check on the status of the trail, call the Coronado National Forest at 520-670-4552.

Box Camp Trail

General Description: *An excellent hike, beginning in pines and ending in saguaro cacti that, with a car shuttle, is nearly all downhill*

Difficulty: *Difficult, mostly continuous steep downhill*

Best Time of Year to Hike: *Spring, fall*

Length: *9.6 miles, one way to Sabino Canyon Tram*

Miles to Trailhead from Speedway/Campbell Intersection: *32.9 miles from intersection to trailhead (does not include leaving a car at Sabino Canyon Visitor Center parking lot)*

Directions to Trailhead from Speedway/Campbell Intersection: *Leave one car at the Sabino Canyon Visitor Center parking lot. Go east on Speedway to Wilmot Road. Turn left on Wilmot Road. Wilmot becomes Tanque Verde. Continue on Tanque Verde until Sabino Canyon Road. Turn left on Sabino Canyon Road and continue until you reach the Visitor Center parking lot, which is on the right. Get in the second car and go back to Tanque Verde. Turn left and drive until you reach the Catalina Highway. Turn left on the Catalina Highway until 0.8 of a mile past Milepost 21. The parking area for the Box Camp Trail is on the left, past Spencer Canyon Road and before Milepost 22. (This car shuttle can be avoided if you can talk someone into driving you up to the trailhead.)*

The Box Camp Trail, built by Frank Webber in 1897, was the first pack route to the high country of the Catalina Mountains. In the days before air-conditioning, Tucsonans rode horses up this trail to summer cabins or camps to escape the summer heat.

The trail, which today connects the Mount Lemmon Highway to the Sabino Canyon tram, is one of the most dramatic trails in the Tucson area. The trail ends after 7.1 miles of nearly continuous downhill in Sabino Basin at 3,700 feet elevation. From Sabino Basin it is 2.5 miles

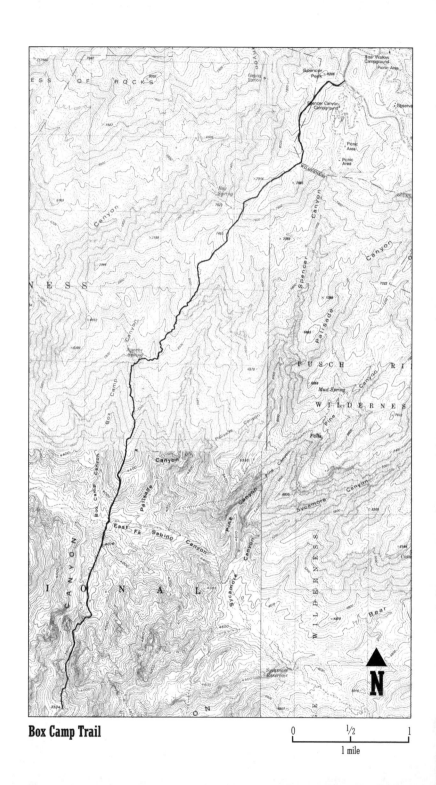

Box Camp Trail

0   1/2   1

1 mile

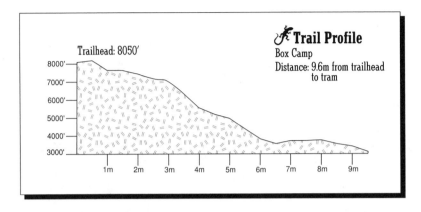

to the head of the Sabino Canyon Road, where, if you make it by 4:00 P.M., you can catch a tram to the Visitor Center parking lot.

Assuming you have arranged transportation, as described in the "Directions to Trailhead" at the beginning of this section, and have enough money for the tram, you're ready to begin. The trail climbs the hill beside the parking area and climbs about 200 yards before leveling out at the powerline. It goes through an old burn area that has regrown and is covered with large ferns, then drops to the west side of the ridge and switchbacks through tall pines to the head of a small stream. The trail continues along the bottom of a ravine, crossing and recrossing the stream several times. As you progress downhill the stream gets larger. If there is water, which there will be in early spring, this is a lovely area, with small waterfalls along the way.

Partway down, a sign indicates that Box Spring is 0.3 of a mile down a side trail to the right. To the left of this sign on a flat area near the top of the ridge, hunters established a camp. They nailed boxes to the trees to protect their food supplies, hence the name Box Camp.

The Box Camp Trail continues down for another 0.25 mile before emerging from the thick pine forest into a more open area with small oaks and manzanita. From here on, the views of the city and the nearby canyons are awesome. Notice Thimble Peak, the prominent thimble-shaped landmark above Sabino Canyon. Before your hike is over, you will be looking up at the Thimble.

The now-rocky trail goes down the top of the ridge between Spencer Canyon on the left and Box Camp Canyon on the right. About halfway down this ridge is an area that looks like it was at one

Hikers pause to take in the view on the Box Camp Trail

time cleared for a helicopter landing. The trail crosses this cleared area and continues down the mountain. There has by now been an almost total change in vegetation. An hour ago you were in a thick, cool pine forest. Now you are hiking through manzanita, oak, and piñon pine.

A fire on this ridge in the summer of 1997 made this portion of the trail hard to follow. Look carefully for cairns and avoid side trails that are blocked by a row of rocks. The trail goes basically straight for about half a mile before bearing to the right or northwest. As you continue to descend, the trail switchbacks steeply down through loose rocks before leveling out in a brushy area. The manzanita is thick and overgrown, making the trail through it easy to follow.

The trail approaches Box Camp Canyon and then turns left, or southeast, and circles the ridge. In about a mile, an interesting rock formation comes into view. It is a long, high sheaf of rocks that has many balanced rocks on top. This is the area known as Apache Spring. The trail crosses a small stream, and there are some large pines to provide shade. Most of the year there will be at least a little water and a number of wildflowers growing in this area. If in fact the Apache Indians did camp here, it is easy to understand why.

Across the stream and on top of a large flat rock you'll find bedrock mortars made by Indian women grinding mesquite beans here. The trail changes in character as it switchbacks its way down through an area covered with large boulders. There are some pine trees and a number of large oaks, breaking for a while the intense sun of the previous part of the trail.

After coming out of this boulder-strewn section, you are close to Box Camp Canyon. Watch carefully for a sharp turn to the right, where the correct route switchbacks steeply down before making a sharp left and turning toward Sabino Canyon. The last time we hiked this section, someone had used a large trail barricade of stones to build a fire in their campsite, and we missed the turn and ended up scrambling down the rocks to rejoin the trail. We hiked the trail again, discovered our error, and rebuilt the barricade. Hopefully, our work has prevented others from making the same mistake.

After descending the switchbacks, the trail circles the ridge and provides a good view of Palisades Canyon, where, if there is enough water, there is a large waterfall. At one point the trail appears to head back uphill and toward the mountains. Don't worry! It soon makes a sharp right and heads directly for Sabino Basin through a short, level area.

This section is more open with an abundance of the nastiest plant in the Catalinas—amole, better known as shindaggers. A series of switchbacks weaves through the shindaggers directly to Sabino Basin. (This section is poorly maintained and the trail easily lost. If you lose your way, bushwhack down the hill to the stream.) Here the saguaros appear again, and by now you are at about the 3,500-foot level.

At the bottom of the switchbacks, you level off briefly and then enter the cool, shady Sabino Basin. Because this is a frequently used camping area, there are a number of trails. Work your way across the creek to the intersection of the Box Camp and East Fork of Sabino Trails. Turn right a few hundred yards to a major trail intersection. Follow Sabino Canyon Trail Number 23 across the creek and out of the basin.

The trail climbs steeply out of Sabino Basin for the first half-mile and then circles the canyon for approximately 1 1/2 miles until coming to the switchbacks that look down on the road. Usually you can see the tram coming up the road. Sometimes it seems to me that this last 0.5 of a mile of switchbacks down to the tram is the longest portion of the trail! When the tram arrives, give the driver your money and hop on board.

Invariably, since you obviously look a little worse for wear, someone will say, "Where did you come from?" It is fun to see their reaction when you say, "Mount Lemmon!"

THE SANTA RITA MOUNTAINS

For nearly three hundred years, mankind has sought the gold and silver in the Santa Rita Mountains. The Spanish were the first to look for the treasures.

In 1736, a large silver strike 75 miles south of Tucson drew a number of Spanish settlers to the area. Many of them came from the Basque region of Spain, and in their explanation of the location of the strike, they referred to it using a Basque term, *aritz onac,* or place of the oaks. An etymologist from the Center for Basque Studies at the University of Nebraska, William A. Douglass, argues that this is the origin of the name, *Arizona.*

The Spanish established a mission at Tumacacori and a presidio at Tubac, both in the shadow of the Santa Ritas. Jesuit priests sent Indian labor to the mines in the Santa Rita Mountains in the 1700s. By the mid-1800s, Apache attacks had forced the abandonment of the Mission and the presidio and the attempts to mine.

When the area became part of the United States with the Gadsden Purchase, attempts were again made at ranching and mining. So rich was the Santa Cruz Valley and the Santa Rita Mountains, that they were the scene of constant battles over ownership. Huge Spanish Land Grants were supposedly to be honored by the Mexican government, and later, by the United States government. Complicating matters were the claims of the heirs of the Baca Float, who claimed the land as replacement for land they had once claimed in New Mexico. The disputes went all the way to the United States Supreme Court and are too complicated to discuss here.

Eventually the heirs of the Baca Float got much of the land in the Santa Cruz Valley, but not without vigorous attempts to claim a large area of the Santa Ritas. In pursuing their claims, two men were sent to survey the mountains. Both were killed by Apaches. Mount Wrightson and Mount Hopkins bear their names.

When most of the Apaches were confined to reservations, mining in the Santa Ritas boomed. Towns grew overnight. Greaterville had a population of 500 by 1879, a public school, a post office, and several saloons. Driving through what remains of the town enroute to a hiking trail, it is hard to visualize that it ever existed. On the north side of the Santa Ritas, the town of Helvetia boasted a population of 400 by 1891. Today all that remains are a few buildings and a cemetery.

Look at the map of the Santa Ritas. The canyons are dotted with the names of mines. Josephine Canyon, Gardner Canyon, and Temporal Gulch all once touted major mining operations. The Agua Caliente Trail passes the old Treasure Vault Mine. Florida Saddle Trail passes the workings of the old Florida Mine. It did not last. By the early 1900s most of the mines had played out. Today Helvetia and Greaterville are ghost towns. The Santa Ritas were made part of the Coronado National Forest in 1908 and are now a National Wilderness Area. The mines are closed forever.

The gold of the Santa Ritas now lies in the hiking trails and beautiful backcountry of the mountains. Although they are the farthest mountains from Tucson, the Santa Ritas provide excellent hiking. The trails that are reached from I-19 and out of Madera Canyon are easiest to access and are primarily the ones included in this section. A complete description of all the hiking trails of the Santa Ritas is available in *Hiker's Guide to the Santa Rita Mountains* by myself and Mike Liebert, also published by Pruett Publishing Company.

Old Baldy Trail

General Description: *A much-used trail to the summit of the highest peak in the Santa Rita Mountains, with spectacular views most of the way and on top*

Difficulty: *Difficult, some areas of exceptionally steep climbing*

Best Time of Year to Hike: *Spring, fall, summer*

Length: *10.8 miles, round-trip*

Miles to Trailhead from Speedway/Campbell Intersection: *43.5 miles*

Directions to Trailhead from Speedway/Campbell Intersection: *Go west on Speedway until you reach the intersection of I-10. Follow I-10 to the intersection of I-19 (the Nogales exit). Follow I-19 to Green Valley. From Green Valley, follow the brown signs to Madera Canyon, getting off at exit 63. Continue following the signs to Madera Canyon, through Continental, to the upper end of the canyon. A sign indicates parking for trails. The Old Baldy trailhead is 0.3 of a mile on a dirt road at the south end of this parking lot.*

One never knows exactly what to expect while hiking this popular Mount Wrightson trail. As I pulled into the parking lot at 7:00 A.M. one Sunday in early June, I was surprised to have difficulty finding a place to park. Then I discovered that a canopy had been set up, and a wedding was in progress. About a mile into the hike I was nearly scared witless by a moving brown object that I thought was a bear. But it was a man and his tripod, both completely covered with camouflage netting. Farther along the trail I met a backpacker with a full-sized guitar attached to his pack. At Bellows Spring I met a man celebrating his sixtieth birthday by taking his poodle, complete with neckerchief, to "sign in" on the summit of Wrightson. (He made it, and I photographed him at the top!) Near Baldy Saddle, I had to dodge a group of runners returning from the summit. One had made it to the top in one hour and thirty-six minutes. It would take me nearly five hours!

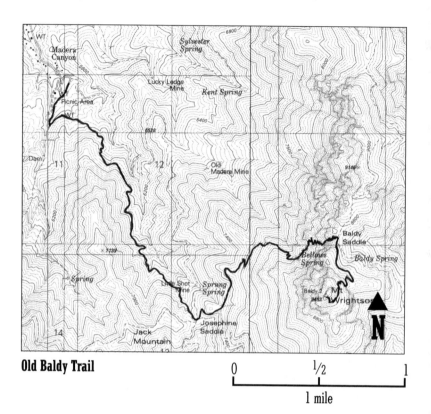

Old Baldy Trail

0   ¹⁄₂   1

1 mile

The Old Baldy Trail to the summit of Mount Wrightson is the most direct route to the 9,453-foot peak, the highest in the Santa Rita Mountain Range. It is also the steepest and most difficult route. The trail name refers to Old Baldy, the original name of Mount Wrightson. It was renamed in memory of William Wrightson, who was killed by Apaches in 1865 as he was attempting to survey this area to establish the claims of the Baca heirs. (His assistant, Gilbert Hopkins, was killed at the same time, and nearby Mount Hopkins is named in his honor.)

The trailhead is 0.4 of a mile up an old road that leaves from the south end of the parking area. The Old Baldy Trail makes a sharp left at a signed intersection. The signs in the Santa Rita Mountains are superior to many signed trails. Made of metal, with the trail name etched through the metal, and attached by pipes set in concrete, they are usually safe from destruction by man and beast!

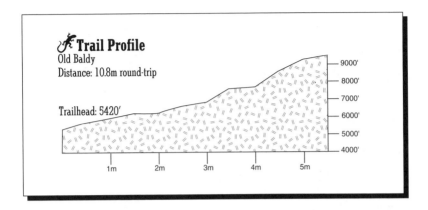

⚕ Trail Profile
Old Baldy
Distance: 10.8m round-trip

Trailhead: 5420'

9000'
8000'
7000'
6000'
5000'
4000'

1m   2m   3m   4m   5m

The trail begins to climb immediately under a canopy of silverleaf oak trees. After about 200 yards there is a large, green water tank to the left. This is the holding tank for the water that supplies the homes and businesses in Madera Canyon.

This is a heavily used trail, and over the years, many persons have shortcut the trail. This unnecessary practice has caused erosion, and in several areas the trail has been rerouted. The old portion of the trail is often covered with dead limbs or otherwise blocked so that the correct route is always easy to follow.

The trail continues to gain elevation quickly. One of the best things about the Old Baldy Trail is the views. You can see Green Valley, the pecan orchards, and the copper mines to the northwest and, as you get higher, the telescopes atop Mount Hopkins to the southwest.

Most of the trail follows the north or east side of the ridge. There are several small drainages that cross the trail that may have water, depending on the time of year you are hiking. After about 1 mile, you cross a large side drainage and then wind around the east side of the hill to an open area that was once used as a helicopter landing pad. Past the open area, the trail reenters the forest, now consisting of oak and ponderosa pine.

After crossing two small drainages, the trail goes slightly downhill, across a large drainage, and climbs along the side of the mountain. In this section, the trail splits, and there is a rather distinct trail that goes to the left. The correct route is the wide trail straight ahead. There are several faint trails in this area that lead down to one of a number of

View of Mount Wrightson from the Old Baldy Trail

secluded camp spots in the ravine. The trail continues along the west side of this ravine and is a lovely area.

Soon the trail begins to switchback steeply. This is one area that has been rerouted, but the main trail is always evident. The switchbacks become longer and end at Josephine Saddle. It will take about 2 hours to reach the saddle.

Josephine Saddle is a crossroads for several trails. The mysterious Josephine of the Santa Ritas has a saddle, a canyon, and a peak named in her honor. The saddle is a beautiful area, covered with tall ponderosa, Apache, Arizona white, and Chihuahua pines. It is a favorite camping area, and it is a rare hike when you do not see a tent set up under a tree.

There are a number of signs in the saddle. The Old Baldy Trail leaves the saddle to the east, past the cross marking the death of three Boy Scouts, who were camped in the vicinity of the saddle on November 15, 1958, when an unusually severe winter storm hit Tucson. The cross and plaque were placed there by their Boy Scout troop. Wreaths and flowers are frequently placed on the cross, which serves, not only as a memorial but as a reminder of the potential danger to those of us who hike and camp on this mountain.

A few yards past the memorial, the Temporal Canyon Trail cuts off to the right. Follow the arrows to the left to Mount Wrightson. The trail to Baldy Saddle switchbacks gradually and, in this section, is sandy and smooth. After the second switchback, you can see the other side of the mountain, including the observatory on Mount Hopkins. The trail goes around the south side of the mountain and climbs gradually. After 0.8 of a mile, you come to a sign indicating the cutoff of the Super Trail to the right. You want to continue left on the Old Baldy Trail. From here Bellows Spring is 1.1 miles; Baldy Saddle, 1.8; and the summit, 2.7. The trail continues to gain elevation, and the views are excellent as it works its way up the mountain.

Soon the trail turns to the right sharply and switchbacks up the mountain. As the switchbacks get steeper, the views get better! There is a short, level area for about 1/4 of a mile, with Mount Wrightson towering above you, before the switchbacks begin again in earnest. Finally the trail levels out in the vicinity of Bellows Spring. Clear, cold water pours into the tank and it is tempting, though unsafe, to take a drink.

Past the spring, the trail is very rocky and exceptionally pretty. It is a brushy trail, with a series of short, rocky switchbacks. A few hundred yards past the spring is a stand of young aspen, but, for the most part, the vegetation consists of thick shrubs. The views up this final section of the trail to Baldy Saddle are excellent. You are about eye level with Mount Hopkins, site of the Smithsonian Institute and University of Arizona's Fred A. Whipple Observatory. To the northwest you can see another famous observatory, Kitt Peak. Baboquivari, the sacred mountain of the Tohono O'odham, is the bald, rounded summit southwest of Kitt Peak. From one vantage point, you can spot your car in the Madera Canyon parking lot.

As the switchbacks approach the saddle, you can see that there has been much shortcutting in the past. Excellent trail reconstruction has been done to discourage the practice and to make the final few switchbacks very evident. The saddle itself is barren compared to Josephine Saddle. Still, the area is much used as a camping spot. Even on the hottest summer day in Tucson, the temperature in the 8,050-foot saddle is delightful.

From the saddle it is 0.9 of a mile to the summit of Mount Wrightson. The trail begins at the south end of the saddle and, for nearly half a mile, is gradual, along the side of the mountain. It goes through tall pines, and the trail is covered with pine needles, making it a welcome change. Of course, this cannot last, and the trail quickly becomes a series of rocky switchbacks with only one break to the top. This rocky, steep trail rounds to the south side of the mountain and climbs to the summit. An excellent interpretive sign explains that this summit was a fire lookout from the 1920s through the 1950s. The remains of the foundation are of a fire lookout cabin that was built in 1928.

The summit of Mount Wrightson has views that, on a clear day, are spectacular. Take a map with you and spend some time picking out the various mountain ranges and the cities that you can see from the top.

Only two things can mar the feeling of accomplishment that you have in climbing this summit. First, if you should be there in June, the ladybugs claim this summit as their own, as do millions of other small insects. Having been warned by hikers coming down from the top, I covered myself with insect repellent, and the bugs loved it! A second problem is the air pollution that too frequently obscures the view.

But on a clear day, standing atop Mount Wrightson, you can understand why people get married in its shadow and carry guitars and poodles to the top. However, it will always be hard for me to understand why anyone runs to the summit!

Super Trail

General Description: *A practically painless way to climb to the summit of Mount Wrightson, this is a gradual trail with some especially beautiful sections*

Difficulty: *Difficult*

Best Time of Year to Hike: *Spring, fall, summer*

Length: *16.4 miles, round-trip*

Miles to Trailhead from Speedway/Campbell Intersection: *43.5 miles*

Directions to Trailhead from Speedway/Campbell Intersection: *Go west on Speedway until you reach the intersection of I-10. Follow I-10 to the intersection of I-19 (the Nogales exit). Follow I-19 to Green Valley. From Green Valley, follow the brown signs to Madera Canyon, getting off at exit 63. Continue following the signs to Madera Canyon, through Continental, to the upper end of the canyon. A sign indicates parking for trails. The Super Trail trailhead is at the north corner of the parking lot.*

The Super Trail begins to the left of the parking area and is marked with an etched metal sign. This exceptionally pretty trail is the easiest, but longest, route to the summit of Mount Wrightson.

The trail parallels the right side of the creek, which has water much of the year. There are nice camping spots beside the creek. The trail passes under tall oaks, juniper pines, and Arizona sycamores. After 1/4 of a mile the trail crosses the creek and heads to the left, in the first of several long, gradual switchbacks. As you turn on the second switchback, there are excellent views of the final goal—Mount Wrightson. The elevation gain is so gradual that almost without realizing it, you are high above the canyon.

The trail goes in and out of shady areas, with several varieties of oak and a few ponderosa pine providing shade. Several side ravines cross the trail. At certain times of year there would be water trickling

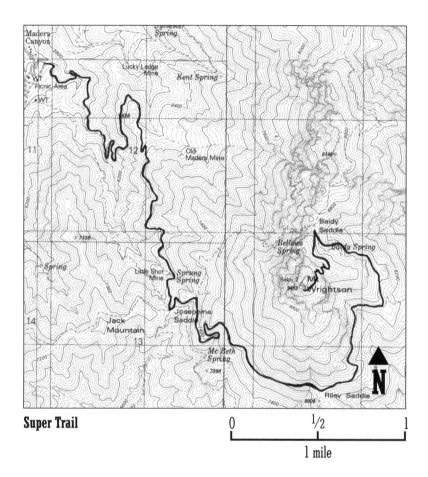

Super Trail

0   ½   1

1 mile

down these ravines. Whatever the time of year, the drainages make very green, pretty areas, often with wildflowers growing. Mount Wrightson pops in and out of view as the trail once again begins to parallel the creek. The creek by now will have small pools in all but the driest of seasons.

After about 1/2 of a mile, the trail again leaves the creek and begins to switchback up the side of the canyon. As you gain in elevation, the views of the valley and the canyon are wider. Green Valley, the dark green of the pecan orchards, and the mines are visible. One long switchback heads north, away from Josephine Saddle, and

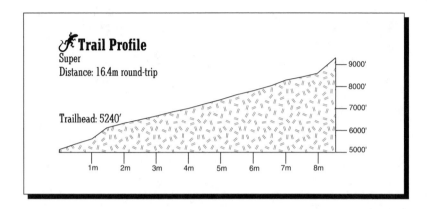

comes to a point of the ridge. Here the views of the valley are especially impressive.

As the trail rounds the ridge and once again heads south toward
Josephine Saddle, it reenters a shady area with ponderosa and
Apache pines and a few spruce. The trail opens up briefly, and now
you can see the observatory on top of Mount Hopkins. Also you can
look down on the Old Baldy Trail headed to Josephine Saddle on the
other side of the canyon.

Past the sign is another exceptionally lovely area. There are pines,
oaks, and an occasional open area. Two-tenths of a mile before
Josephine Saddle, is Sprung Spring. A round metal tank with water
piped in is a welcome sight. It is always running, and although it
should be purified before drinking, it is nice to know that this permanent source of water is available. The trees surrounding the spring are
tall, and the vegetation is lush. This is a great area for wildlife spotting,
especially in early evening. A faint trail going downhill from the spring
leads to the Little Shot Mine, should you be interested in a side exploration. The opening has been partially cemented for safety.

Past the spring the trail switchbacks quickly into Josephine Saddle, coming out right at the sign that marks the deaths of three Boy
Scouts, who were camped in the vicinity of the saddle on November
15, 1958, when an unusually severe winter storm hit Tucson. At this
crossroads it is possible to leave the Super Trail and continue your ascent of Mount Wrightson by the Old Baldy Trail. This would shorten
the hike considerably, but add greatly to the steepness. I'll assume that
you plan to go all the way to Baldy Saddle via the Super Trail. To do

Memorial on the Super Trail

this, turn left at the signed intersection, following the arrow to Mount Wrightson. The trail switchbacks to the left and then quickly to the right. Continue up this switchback for approximately 200 yards to another signed intersection. Follow the sign to the right to continue your climb to Mount Wrightson via the Super Trail. From this point it is another 4.2 miles to the summit. The ascent is so gradual that this is practically a painless way to attain Baldy Saddle. Unfortunately, there is no painless way to make it to the summit of Mount Wrightson!

The trail climbs in a series of long, easy switchbacks at first and crosses a rocky area. From all along this portion of the trail there are excellent views of Mount Hopkins. The observatory atop Mount Hopkins is a joint venture of the University of Arizona and the Smithsonian Institution.

As the trail winds around the mountain, there are a couple of spots where the trail crosses rock falls. For about a mile the trail goes through a grassy area with clumps of grass and a few pine and small oak. The basic plan of the trail is to go around the south side of Mount Wrightson. A trail cuts off to the right across Riley Saddle to Josephine Peak. You should continue straight ahead. Past the trail intersection, the trail continues to gradually work its way around the mountain, coming to the drainage that comes down from Mount Wrightson. Here are large rocks, a large alligator juniper, and a huge ponderosa pine. Farther up the drainage, you can see a stand of aspen. The trail leaves this drainage and continues through an open area to a trail intersection. The trail to the right leads off to Gardner Canyon. You should continue left and around Mount Wrightson.

Soon you leave the open area and come into a beautiful area. Several long switchbacks lead through tall ponderosas and Douglas fir trees to Baldy Saddle. Right before reaching Baldy Spring, there is an oft-used campsite with logs for sitting and the ever-present fire ring. Almost immediately past this campsite is Baldy Spring. The tank is nearly always full, and the water can be used if it is purified. In half a mile from the spring, you are at Baldy Saddle. The Super Trail ends at Baldy Saddle, and you turn left and join the Old Baldy Trail to the summit.

You can return from Mount Wrightson down the Super Trail, the Old Baldy Trail, or a combination of both. If the entire hike is done on the Super Trail, it is a total of 16.4 miles. That makes for a very long hike, regardless of how gradual it is. Hikers soon learn the combination that most suits their hiking style.

Kent Spring–Bog Springs Loop Trail

General Description: *A loop trail past three springs through a riparian area*

Difficulty: *Moderate, some areas of steep climbing*

Best Time of Year to Hike: *Spring, fall, winter*

Length: *5.4 mile loop*

Miles to Trailhead from Speedway/Campbell Intersection: *42 miles*

Directions to Trailhead from Speedway/Campbell Intersection: *Go west on Speedway until you reach the intersection of I-10. Follow I-10 east to the intersection of I-19 (the Nogales exit). Follow I-19 to Green Valley. From Green Valley, follow the brown signs to Madera Canyon, getting off at exit 63. Go left under I-19, following the signs to Madera Canyon, through Continental, to a parking area on the left on the main road, just past the sign for the Bog Springs Campground. This parking area is called Madera Trailhead and has rest rooms and a few picnic tables. A sign in the middle of the parking area indicates the Bog Springs Campground. Follow this trail to the beginning of the Kent Spring–Bog Springs Loop Trail.*

The Kent Spring–Bog Springs Loop is one of the prettiest hikes in the Santa Rita Mountains. A series of springs creates an unusually lush area that attracts a large number of birds and wildlife. Large Arizona sycamore and walnut trees provide a canopy that invites you to relax and spend the better part of a day before returning to the arid environment of southeastern Arizona.

Follow the trail from the Madera Trailhead, along the right side of a deep ravine, until reaching an old road, about 0.2 of a mile. Turn

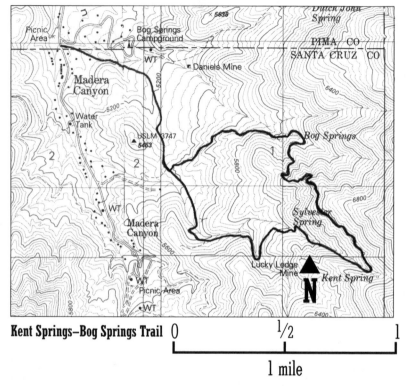

Kent Springs–Bog Springs Trail

0   1/2   1

1 mile

right and follow the road approximately 0.5 of a mile to the trailhead.
A sign on the left indicates the beginning of the Kent Spring–Bog
Springs Loop Trail. From this point it is 0.8 of a mile to Bog Springs
and 2 miles to Kent Springs. You will return to this spot. You may go
first to Bog Springs and then circle to Kent Spring and back to the
trailhead, or reverse the direction. I prefer to hike to Bog Springs first,
so the following directions will describe the loop in that direction.

Past the sign the trail is no longer a road, but a narrow, smooth,
and sandy path. To the north and northwest, the views of Kitt Peak,
the copper mines, Green Valley, and surrounding communities stand
out as you gain in elevation. After climbing steadily for nearly a mile,
the trail drops into Bog Springs. There is a concrete tank and a spigot
for water a short distance beyond the tank. Webster defines *bog* as
"wet, spongy ground." This area comes as close to that definition as
is possible in southeastern Arizona. The reed-like horsetail grows in

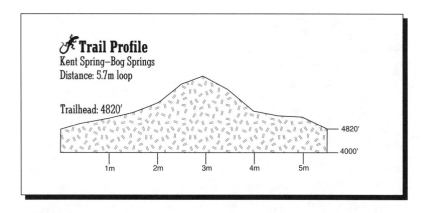

Trail Profile
Kent Spring–Bog Springs
Distance: 5.7m loop

Trailhead: 4820'

4820'

4000'

1m   2m   3m   4m   5m

abundance. There are huge Arizona sycamores, many of them with hollowed-out trunks that would be large enough to shelter a person caught in a storm. Beyond the spring are two stone-covered tanks, and farther up the canyon, there are several small, concrete tanks. There are huge fir trees, Arizona walnut trees, and again many Arizona sycamores.

As the trail leaves the spring and climbs the side of the canyon, there is an almost total change in vegetation. What was a green and lush canyon becomes a scrub oak-covered, dry ridge. The trail switchbacks as it climbs to Kent Spring. At the point of the ridge, there are excellent views of Mount Wrightson. Past this point, a few more switchbacks, and you are on top of the ridge. A large log, worn smooth by many resting hikers, invites you to sit and take in the views. Now Baboquivari and Kitt Peaks are both visible.

Past the log, the trail is fairly level along the side of the ridge, with some moderate uphill. Several points in this area are rocky, and the shale covering the trail, in combination with the narrowness of the trail, makes it easy to fall. As the trail goes back into the forest, walking becomes easy again. As you approach Kent Spring, huge Arizona sycamores again dominate the scene. There is a small stream that runs most of the year. The area is not quite as green as Bog Springs, but it is very close. Across the stream is a round, stone tank that is Kent Spring.

This spring was most likely named for W.H.B. Kent, a supervisor in the Tumacacori Division of the Forest Service from 1904 until 1908. Kent was a maverick ranger, wearing a bandanna instead of the

Hiker tests the water at Kent Spring

regulation Stetson, and holding meetings near a spring in the Santa Ritas, where he read poetry to his charges. His fondness for whiskey earned him the nickname "Whiskey High Balls" Kent. By 1911, Kent was "eased" out of the Forest Service and, after serving in France during World War I, he moved to California to write Western novels. His *The Tenderfoot* and *Range Rider* were published by New York's Macmillan and Company. Copies may be found at the University of Arizona Library, Special Collections section.

At the spring, the trail goes sharply right and becomes a jeep road. It is all downhill from here, except for a few short portions near the end. The road follows the stream down the mountain and is lovely. After about 1/2 of a mile, you come to Sylvester Spring, which consists of a large concrete tank and two smaller tanks. This spring probably bears the name of Art and Anna Sylvester, who had a summer cabin in Madera Canyon in the 1930s.

Past the spring, the road is uphill for a very short time and is no longer rocky. For much of the way the road follows the left of the stream. At a pipeline, the trail crosses the stream and, depending on the time of year, can require wading. This entire portion along the stream is beautiful, with tall trees and, hopefully, the sound of water running. I think it would be an unusual hike if you did not see deer along this stream.

As the trail approaches the end, it becomes sandy, as it pulls away from the stream and out into the open. Look carefully for the turnoff to the Madera trailhead. It's right before the road drops steeply into a wash.

Dutch John Spring Trail

General Description: *A short, pleasant hike, through an evergreen oak forest to two springs*

Difficulty: *Moderate*

Best Time of Year to Hike: *Spring, fall, winter*

Length: *3.6 miles, round-trip*

Miles to Trailhead from Speedway/Campbell Intersection: *42 miles*

Directions to Trailhead from Speedway/Campbell Intersection: *Drive west on Speedway to I-10. Turn left under the interstate and get on I-10 headed east (El Paso) until you reach the intersection with I-19 (Nogales exit). Follow I-19 through Green Valley to exit 63. At exit 63 turn left under the Interstate, following the signs to Madera Canyon, through Continental, to the parking lot on the left on the main road, immediately past the turnoff to the Bog Springs Campground. There are rest rooms and several picnic areas. The sign at the parking lot says, "Madera Trailhead."*

The Santa Rita Mountains hold many mysteries. One involves "Dutch John." Surely someone didn't just find this spring and say, "Why don't we name this Dutch John Spring?" There must be more to the story.

A search of the Santa Cruz County Courthouse records and the Pimeria Alta Historical Society library in Nogales turned up a John Tannenbaum, a man of German descent, born in the German section of Fredericksburg, Texas, who moved to the Patagonia area after, some say, having killed a man in Texas.

Tannenbaum worked on ranches in the Santa Ritas and was known locally as "the Dutchman." In 1926, while working as a cook for the 7V Ranch roundup, Tannenbaum killed a man who told him to bridle his horse. According to Frank Seibold's *Tales From Sonoita*, Tannenbaum told the man he "did not do bridles." A heated argument

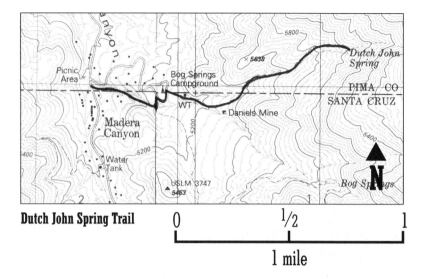

Dutch John Spring Trail

0        $^1\!/_2$ 1

1 mile

followed and the man never made another such request (or any other request for that matter). Nothing links John Tannenbaum to Dutch John Spring, but it makes a good story!

The hike to the spring begins on the northeast side of the parking area, between the rest rooms and the first picnic table, where a small sign says, "Bog Spgs. C/G." Up the trail and on the right are the foundations of what was once a cabin. Many of the cabins in this area were removed by the Forest Service when their leases expired. It was a controversial decision not to renew the leases, and at least one owner had to be forcibly evicted.

A trail cuts off to the right to the Santa Rita Lodge. Your route is to continue ahead to the Bog Springs Campground. The trail follows the right side of the drainage for about 0.3 of a mile, to a signed intersection. Turn left on what was once a jeep road that drops steeply down into a drainage. Follow the dirt road for a short distance to the paved road. Turn right on this road and proceed uphill for about 410 feet, and you will be at the center of the Bog Springs Campground. (It is possible to park here for this hike if you wish to pay a $5.00 parking fee.) A large sign explains the rules of the campsite and serves as a self-service pay station. Directly across the road from the sign is a picnic table. Steps lead up to this site, and, as you walk on the trail between the two picnic tables, you will see a sign indicating the Dutch John Trail.

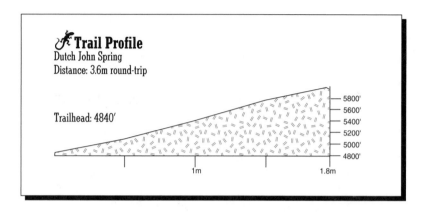

𖠿 Trail Profile

Dutch John Spring
Distance: 3.6m round-trip

Trailhead: 4840'

5800'
5600'
5400'
5200'
5000'
4800'

1m   1.8m

The trail begins to climb, passing two very large water tanks on the right. Immediately past the water tanks is a fence and a "people only" pass-through metal gate. The trail is at first a gradual climb, with the canyon on the right. The canyon is filled with Arizona sycamore and several varieties of oak trees. Evergreen oaks—silverleaf, Arizona white, and Emory—are a trademark of this trail and grow unusually large because of the abundance of water here.

A sign marks the wilderness boundary, as you pass under a canopy of the beautiful oaks. Past the boundary marker, the trail gets steeper, and the leaves on the trail make it slippery. These evergreen oaks do lose their leaves, but unlike the deciduous Gambel's oak, new leaves immediately replace old ones, thus the term *live oaks.*

In about 0.6 of a mile after leaving the campground, a path leads to the left, to what is marked with a metal sign that says, "Dutch John Spring." A small bathtub-shaped tank provides water for wildlife. It is a pleasant area with large Arizona sycamores interspersed with oaks and junipers. Although this spring is marked "Dutch John Spring," it is not indicated as such on any maps. Let's keep looking!

The trail continues up the hill and is at times confusing as it crosses and recrosses the drainage. If you question whether you are on the trail, retrace your steps to make certain you didn't miss a turn. You'll pass several level campsites, some with handbuilt stone foundations. Perhaps this was a summer camp for some heat-weary Tucsonans in the early 1900s. Past these sites, the trail climbs even more steeply, and for a few hundred yards, comes out into the open, and there are good views of Pete Mountain to the southwest. As you near

The "first" Dutch John Spring

the top of the drainage, the trail turns sharply to the right. The trail once again enters the oak forest and becomes quite steep. The trail hugs the right side of the ridge and is slippery. As the trail drops slightly down into a drainage and enters a lush area, you will see a partially broken cement catchment. This is where maps of the area indicate Dutch John Spring is located.

Perhaps a tired trail crew worker got tired of carrying the heavy metal sign and put it at the wrong spring. Regardless of whether this is Dutch John Spring or the site back down the trail is Dutch John Spring, both areas are beautiful. Water trickles in the stream and out of the springs. Hummingbirds dart about, and blue jays and cardinals can usually be seen in the trees. In the evening, deer and javelina surely frequent this area. Maybe, if you close your eyes, you'll see old Dutch John himself, looking for the spring that bears his name.

Agua Caliente (Vault Mine) Josephine Saddle Loop Trail

General Description: *A little-used trail past an old mine that provides outstanding views*

Difficulty: *Difficult, some areas of exceptionally steep climbing*

Best Time of Year to Hike: *Spring, fall, summer*

Length: *6.1 miles—Old Baldy return; 7.4 miles—Super Trail return*

Miles to Trailhead from Speedway/Campbell Intersection: *43.5 miles*

Directions to Trailhead from Speedway/Campbell Intersection: *Go west on Speedway until you reach the intersection of I-10. Follow I-10 to the intersection of I-19 (the Nogales exit). Remain on I-19 until you reach Green Valley. Follow the brown signs to Madera Canyon, getting off at exit 63. Follow the signs to Madera Canyon. In the upper part of Madera Canyon, a sign indicates parking for trails. The Agua Caliente (Vault Mine) Trail is 0.6 of a mile on a dirt road at the south end of this parking lot.*

"Tips for Hikers," published by the Friends of Madera Canyon and available at the parking area, does not recommend hiking the Agua Caliente (Vault Mine) Trail. The directional sign placed at the intersection warns that the trail is VERY STEEP. True, the trail does climb 1,400 vertical feet in 0.6 of a mile, and it is VERY STEEP, but, as a loop trail through Josephine Saddle, it is one of the prettiest hikes leading out of Madera Canyon.

The Vault Mine Trail begins 0.6 of a mile up the old road that leads south from the parking area. At 0.3 of a mile, you come to the first trail intersection. To the left is the Old Baldy Trail to Josephine Saddle. Continue up the road, following the sign to Agua Caliente Trail, the one indicated on the sign as being a "Very Steep Trail." The old road parallels

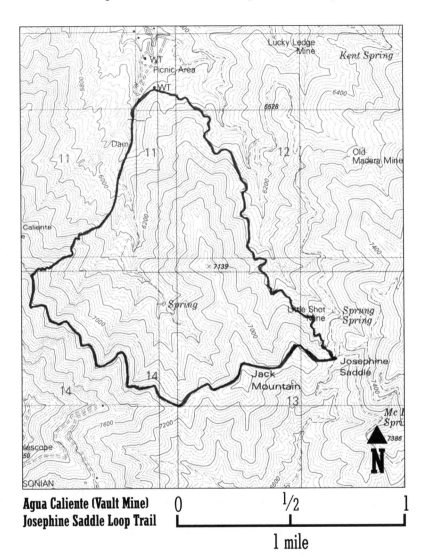

**Agua Caliente (Vault Mine)
Josephine Saddle Loop Trail**

0   1/2   1

1 mile

Madera Creek. Usually there is some water flowing in the stream. Tall
Arizona sycamores and several varieties of oak shade the area. Over
two hundred species of birds have been spotted in Madera Canyon, including the rare, colorful elegant trogon. Once, I encountered a birder
running up this trail in search of a trogon!

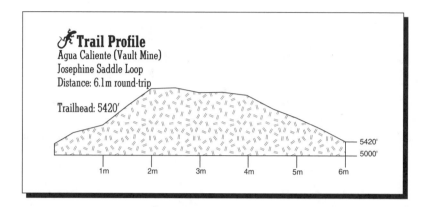

🦎 Trail Profile
Agua Caliente (Vault Mine)
Josephine Saddle Loop
Distance: 6.1m round-trip

Trailhead: 5420'

As the road steepens, keep looking for a side trail on the right that crosses the stream. This area is used heavily, and there are many side trails leading down to the stream. The correct trail crosses Madera Creek and passes to the right of a large silverleaf oak tree. In about 200 yards, a sign indicates that the Agua Caliente Trail is to the right. From here, it is 3.2 miles to Josephine Saddle.

Past the sign, the trail soon follows a ledge far above Madera Creek. This is a beautiful area, with large oaks and pines. It is level only briefly, before beginning a series of steep switchbacks. After the first set of switchbacks, the trail comes to an open area, and you can see the Catalina Mountains and part of Tucson, before the trail again switchbacks up the hill. Unfortunately, there has been a lot of short-cutting on the trail. It is hard to understand why anyone would want to shortcut when the trail is already very steep.

As the trail rounds to the east side of the mountain, it opens up, and the trees are not as thick. It is again very rocky and steep. After 0.6 of a mile and a 1400-foot elevation gain, you come to an abandoned mine tunnel.

This is not the Treasure Vault Mine, as the trail name would suggest, but the Lead Prospect Mine. The Treasure Vault Mine is on the other side of the saddle and can be reached by continuing on the Agua Caliente Trail. Mining in this area dates to the arrival of the Jesuit fathers in the 1680s, who used Indian labor to search for gold and silver. However, by the time of the Gadsden Purchase in 1853, when this area became part of the United States, Apache raids made mining too dangerous. It was not until after the Civil War that American miners once again entered the area.

The Lead Prospect Mine on the Agua Caliente (Vault Mine) Trail

The trail beyond the mine, with the exception of the first 200 yards, is exceptionally steep and rocky. At 1.2 miles you come to a signed intersection. Turn left to Josephine Saddle. Now the steep part of the trail is over, as it circles the mostly open, northeast side of the mountain. Although there are a few steep dropoffs and several areas where the trail crosses rockfalls, the trail is a joy to hike from here to Josephine Saddle.

During the first part of this section of trail, there are some very large oak trees. It must have been a good year for acorns, because there are hundreds of tiny oak trees along the trail, so thick that in several places I found myself putting my foot down, hoping that there was not a rattler in there shading itself! The trail goes in and out of cover, under huge box elder and pine trees. In spring, the pink blossoms of locust trees lend a pleasant fragrance to the air. There is also a section of large, beautiful aspen, one of the few areas of aspen in the Santa Ritas.

After you have been hiking for about 1 1/2 miles, there is a trail to the right that eventually goes up to Mount Hopkins. It is interesting to go the hundred yards or so to the top of the ridge. The road up Mount Hopkins is visible, as are several buildings and what looks like the back of one of the telescopes. There are several huge alligator juniper trees, including one at least 6 feet in diameter.

Past this lookout point, the trail goes downhill gradually and comes to a short saddle, before once again gaining in elevation. There is an open area covered with ferns that looks like it was once a burn area. Past this burn area, the trail reenters the woods and goes downhill gradually until it reaches Josephine Saddle.

As you will see, Josephine Saddle is a crossroads for many trails, which makes it possible to come up with any number of loops. For this particular loop, you may return to the parking area via the Old Baldy Trail (page 165, 2.2 miles) or the Super Trail (page 172, 3.7 miles). The choice depends on the condition of your legs and the amount of time you have allotted for hiking.

Elephant Head
Hiking/Biking Trail

General Description: *A rambling hike across the foothills of the Santa Rita Mountains, from Madera Canyon to the base of Elephant Head*

Difficulty: *Moderate*

Best Time of Year to Hike: *Winter*

Length: *14 miles, round-trip*

Miles to Trailhead from Speedway/Campbell Intersection: *41.5 miles*

Directions to Trailhead from Speedway/Campbell Intersection: *Drive west on Speedway to I-10. Turn left under the interstate and get on I-10 headed east (El Paso), until you reach the intersection with I-19 (Nogales exit). Follow I-19, through Green Valley, to exit 63. At exit 63 turn left under the Interstate, following the signs to Madera Canyon, through Continental, to the Proctor parking area, which is on the right at the entrance to Madera Canyon.*

Pick a warm winter day and head for the Elephant Head Hiking/Biking Trail, from Madera Canyon, to the base of Elephant Head. You'll find a pleasant wander, with little elevation gain or loss across the foothills of the Santa Rita Mountains, which provides outstanding views of this rugged country, dominated from this perspective by the massive Elephant Head formation.

From the Proctor parking area, begin on the barrier-free trail that leaves from the southwest corner of the lot just past the rest rooms. Walk about 0.2 of a mile on the asphalt surface to the intersection with Proctor Road, which is unpaved. Turn right on the road. If you prefer, you can drive a mile down the road and park just before the road turns into a trail, but the walk is pleasant, crossing Madera Creek, through a stand of huge Arizona sycamores.

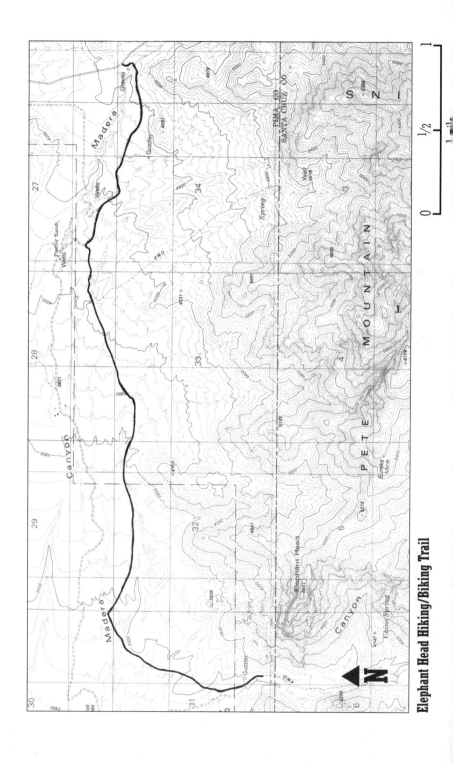

Elephant Head Hiking/Biking Trail

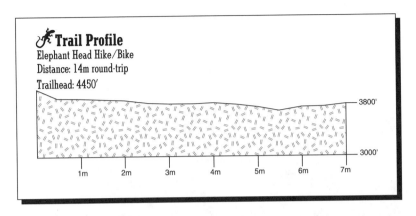

🦎 Trail Profile
Elephant Head Hike/Bike
Distance: 14m round-trip
Trailhead: 4450'

As you go along the road, note the views of Elephant Head. When you finish this hike, you will be at the base of Elephant Head, in Chino Basin. There are sweeping views to the northwest of Babo-quivari, the thimble-shaped peak that is the sacred mountain of the Tohono O'odham Indians. To the north are the copper mines and a huge tailings pond that reflects the sun at certain angles. And behind you, to the south, are the majestic Santa Rita Mountains, topped by Mount Wrightson and Mount Hopkins.

This is spectacular country, and it is easy to understand why several pioneer families homesteaded in this area in the late 1800s. Proctor Road is named for Charles R. Proctor, son of Charles A. Proctor, who first came to southeastern Arizona in 1885. Charles R. Proctor homesteaded along this road in 1919, and today the ranch is still being operated by his descendants.

In an excellent article called "Valley of Iron," in the autumn 1993 *Journal of Arizona History,* Proctor's daughter, Margaret Proctor Redondo, tells of growing up on the Proctor Ranch. She gives an account of her father's skill at making moonshine during prohibition days and has in her possession her father's still, which is pictured in the article. Maps show the location of the Proctor Ranch.

The trail is well-marked by slender, brown signs that indicate that this trail is accessible to hikers, mountain bikers, and horseback riders. It first uses a network of Forest Roads, leaving Proctor Road to turn left on FR 781 and quickly left again on FR 4074, before coming to a gate that prohibits further driving. Motorized vehicles, including ATVs, are not permitted after the trail passes through the gate.

Elephant Head Hiking/Biking Trail

Although the elevation gain and loss is minimal on this trail, it is not by any means level. It climbs in and out of washes, at times steeply. One section is filled with tall Mexican blue oaks and offers a sharp contrast to most of the trail, which is out in the open. Every time I see trees growing like this, I am reminded of an old Arizona story. Back in territorial days, Arizona frequently tried to gain statehood, only to be blocked for various reasons. Finally, in an impassioned plea, the Arizona delegate says, "All Arizona needs is water and some good people." The response? "That's all Hell needs!" This little story has nothing to do with hiking, but, it points out a desert truth—a little water makes a lot of difference.

This is also an excellent hike to observe the "small stuff." Cardinals and jays dart between the trees. Intricate bird nests adorn the large chain cholla. Javelina and mule deer browse on the prickly pear. The javelina bites leave the prickly pear pads shredded, as they pull pieces off. The deer, by contrast, take neat little bites. Under the cacti and trees, you'll find large pack rat nests that reveal the industriousness of these tiny creatures.

About halfway to Elephant Head is an unusual shrine that appears to be dedicated to a fallen mountain biker. Decorated with bicycle parts, flowers, candles, and gourds, the shrine is comparable to those along Arizona's highways that remember car accident victims.

As you approach Elephant Head, the trail climbs a ridge and, for about a mile, heads directly away from Elephant Head. Just when you think you may be going toward the interstate, the trail turns and heads directly for Elephant Head. It joins FR 4073 and goes into Chino Basin.

It takes two and one-half to three hours to reach this point, which is the turnaround spot for this hike. Should you be feeling particularly ambitious, continue up Chino Basin to the adobe ruins of Elephant Head Mill. It is even possible to arrange key swaps, by leaving a second vehicle at the Elephant Head/Little Elephant Head trailhead on FR 183.

Elephant Head towers high above you, as you reach the end of the day's hike. Although from this angle it seems impossible, there is a route to the top of Elephant Head. *Hiker's Guide to the Santa Rita Mountains,* also published by Pruett Publishing Company, gives detailed directions for making the climb.

Many stories surround Elephant Head. Apaches were said to have forced their victims to climb to the top of the rock formation, before they tossed them off to their death. Legend has it that Jesuit priests buried gold in caves around Elephant Head, leading to many treasure-hunting expeditions over the years. Another story tells that some people from India filled animal hide sacks that were in the shape of human torsos with gold and precious stones and buried them in secret caverns. During the 1940s, a Mr. and Mrs. Darrall, claiming to have a map to the caverns, built a small house at the foot of Elephant Head and spent five years looking for the treasure. They even installed a cable to lift supplies and equipment to the top of Elephant Head. As yet, no one has found the buried treasure of Elephant Head. I think the real treasure is in a warm winter day, a clear blue sky, and good friends to make the trek along the Elephant Head Hiking/Biking Trail.

Agua Caliente Trail

General Description: *A scenic,little-used trail to a beautiful saddle*

Difficulty: *Difficult*

Best Time of Year to Hike: *Spring, fall*

Length: *4.4 miles, round-trip*

Miles to Trailhead from Speedway/Campbell Intersection: *44 miles*

Directions to Trailhead from Speedway/Campbell Intersection: *Go west on Speedway until you reach the intersection of I-10. Follow I-10 east (El Paso) until you reach the intersection of I-19 (the Nogales exit). Follow I-19 south, past Green Valley, to the Canoa exit, number 56. Turn left under the highway, following signs to Elephant Head Road. At the intersection, turn right to Elephant Head Road, a distance of 3 miles. Turn left on Elephant Head Road. After you cross the Santa Cruz River and the railroad tracks, watch carefully on the right for Mount Hopkins Road. Turn right on Mount Hopkins Road for 5.5 miles to Forest Service Road 183. The sign will say, "Agua Caliente Canyon and KMSB." Turn left on Forest Service Road 183 and continue for 3.2 miles. The trailhead is on the right, a little over 1/2 of a mile after the road crosses Agua Caliente Creek and begins the steep climb to the television towers. A large metal sign by the side of the road marks the beginning of the Agua Caliente Trail. There is not a parking area, but there is room to pull your vehicle off to the side of the road. Although a high-clearance vehicle is best for this road, driving carefully in a passenger car will get you there.*

*A*gua Caliente—hot water in Spanish—is the name given to the canyon between Mount Hopkins and Elephant Head. The spring that gives the canyon its name is at the mouth of the canyon and, according to a geothermal survey by the Arizona Geological Survey, is more warm than hot, never rising above 100 degrees. Although it is

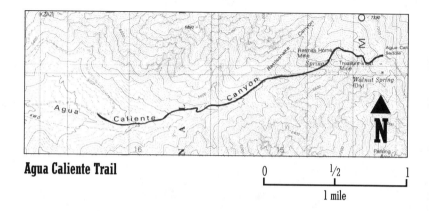

Agua Caliente Trail

0   ¹⁄₂   1

1 mile

a long drive to the trailhead to hike a relatively short trail, the hike to Agua Caliente Saddle provides a different perspective on the Santa Ritas and gives the hiker a better understanding of the size of the range.

The trail goes along the north side of Agua Caliente Canyon and is at times rocky. Most of the year there will be some water running in the canyon. There are excellent views of the Smithsonian Institution's Fred A. Whipple Observatory on top of Mount Hopkins.

As the trail winds its way out of the canyon, the vegetation changes to varieties of oaks and pines, and the rocky trail gives way to a smooth, pine-covered surface. This is temporary, because the nature of the trail changes quickly to a rocky climb past the workings of the Treasure Vault Mine. Located in 1899, this mine was operated by the Santa Rita Mining Company. If you scramble down to explore the remains of the operation, you'll find two shafts (vertical openings) and one adit (horizontal opening). They were all flooded the last time I hiked this trail.

The climb past the mine is steep. As the trail bears right and crosses a small drainage, the vegetation changes to include Apache and ponderosa pines. Views open up to the northwest and include the 7,661-foot Pete Mountain, which can be reached from Agua Caliente Saddle. Finally, a last, long switchback past an exceptionally large alligator juniper leads to the saddle.

From this saddle a bushwhacking route leads to the Mount Hopkins Observatory. There is also a trail to Pete Mountain. Also, it is 0.8

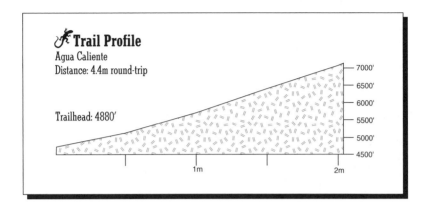

✿ Trail Profile

Agua Caliente
Distance: 4.4m round-trip

Trailhead: 4880′

of a mile of gradual uphill to the intersection of the Vault Mine Trail. From this intersection, the Agua Caliente Trail continues 2.2 miles to Josephine Saddle. This portion of the Agua Caliente Trail is described in the Vault Mine Trail description. By carefully studying a trail map of the Santa Ritas, you can work out any number of hiking combinations.

View from beginning of Agua Caliente Trail

Florida Saddle Trail

General Description: *A steep hike through a beautiful canyon, along open hillsides, to a thickly forested saddle*

Difficulty: *Difficult, some areas of exceptionally steep climbing*

Best Time of Year to Hike: *Spring, fall*

Length: *10.4 miles, round-trip*

Miles to Trailhead from Speedway/Campbell Intersection: *42.6 miles*

Directions to Trailhead from Speedway/Campbell Intersection: *Go west on Speedway until you reach the intersection of I-10. Follow I-10 to the intersection of I-19 (the Nogales exit). Get on I-19 to Green Valley. In Green Valley, follow the brown signs to Madera Canyon, getting off at exit 63 and continuing to follow the signs to Madera Canyon. Seven miles past Continental, the Box Canyon Road (Forest Service Road 62) turns left. This road is unpaved, but is suitable for passenger cars. When the road splits, follow the sign to Florida Work Center. Trailhead parking is on the left.*

This trail is not pronounced "Florida," as in the state, but "Flor-eee-da," as in Spanish for *flowery*. Miners working here in the 1880s probably named the canyon for its abundant, beautiful flowers. Rarely will you meet a fellow hiker on this trail, because most hikers approach the Santa Ritas from Madera Canyon.

A Charles Robinson owned nine claims in this area in the 1880s. By the early 1900s, the Florida Mine had three 50- to 100-foot tunnels and shallow shafts. The miners lived in Robinson Camp, near a spring, and received their mail from the nearby boomtown of Helvetia. Production at the mine did not meet expectations, and only 140 tons of copper ore were ever produced.

From the parking area, the trail immediately crosses the creek and starts up a road. It parallels a fence on a narrow rocky trail, past two rectangular concrete stock tanks. As the trail climbs a brief rise, the

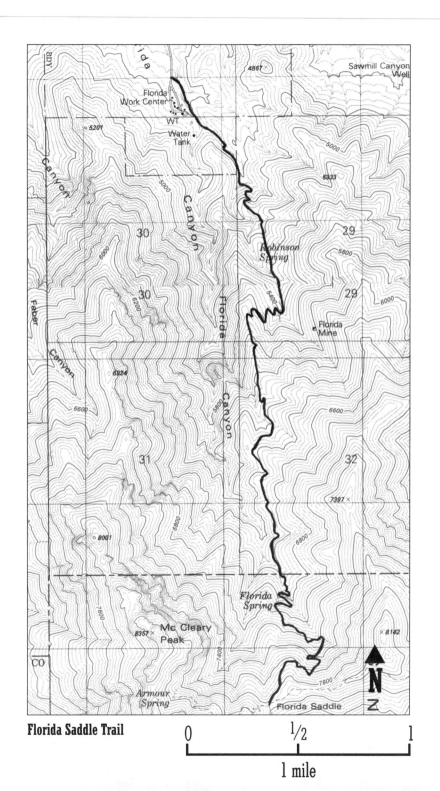

Florida Saddle Trail

0   1/2   1

1 mile

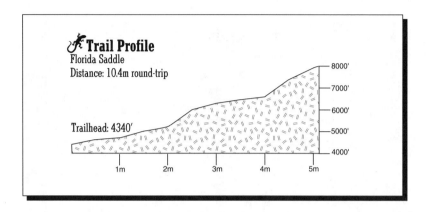

🦎**Trail Profile**
Florida Saddle
Distance: 10.4m round-trip

Trailhead: 4340′

8000′
7000′
6000′
5000′
4000′

1m 2m 3m 4m 5m

buildings of the Florida Work Center and the Santa Rita Experimental Station, administered by the University of Arizona, under a lease from the State of Arizona, can be seen on your right. This is an unusual area in that the tall trees growing in the canyon on the right contrast sharply with the huge prickly pear cacti and ocotillo on the left.

In 0.3 of a mile you reach a hinged gate, which is the entry to the Coronado National Forest. Across the creek bed is a sign indicating the beginning of the Florida Saddle Trail. From this point, it is 4.2 miles to Florida Saddle. The trail crosses the stream several times, but most of the year, the stream will be dry. There are several rock check dams wired together with fencing material, which occasionally back up pools of water. An empty round stock tank is on the right of the trail.

After not quite a mile, the trail leaves the creek bed and begins to climb out of the bottom of the canyon. As you climb, you begin to get good views of the valley to the north. At the top of another rise is a round stock tank, this one very much in use, because cattle graze in this area.

The switchbacks level out, and the now-rocky trail continues uphill. The vegetation changes to include piñon pines and alligator junipers. The trail drops down slightly into an area known as Robinson Spring. At even the driest time of year, there will be some moisture in the area and many colorful flowers.

Past the spring, the trail enters a lovely area, with tall Arizona sycamores and a canopy of oak trees. It continues to climb under the trees for about 1/4 of a mile. Past this area, the trail switchbacks up to the top of what appears to be a tailing pile from the old mines. For

A pleasant campsite in Florida Saddle

a brief period, the trail levels off and enters some fir trees. Past this fir tree section, the trail opens up again and switchbacks steeply up the side of the hill. The trail is rocky and at times hard to climb. It tops a ridge to an area that has been cleared. Here a trail leads off to the right to a campsite. The correct route is uphill, to the left. The views from this cleared area are excellent, both into the valley and into Florida Canyon, to the west.

After another quarter of a mile of climbing through manzanita and oak, the trail reenters a shady area with some tall pine and fir trees. A partially buried water pipe follows the trail, which soon drops down into a grassy ravine. This is near Florida Spring, where most of the year, there will be some water trickling. Flowers also grow in abundance here. Across the drainage and around the basin, the trail enters a section with huge fir trees.

From here to the saddle, the trail is a joy to hike, in the shade of huge fir and pine trees, even though the switchbacks are some of the longest I've ever traversed. You pass an area that has some big logs and boards used for seats, which has been used as a camping area. A final, long switchback to the right brings you to the saddle. A beautiful spot used for camping, this saddle is the intersection for several trails and is often used as a connecting loop with the Josephine Saddle trails. Bring a hammock, stretch it between two trees, and rest your legs for the trip down. This is almost as good as it gets.

Selected Readings

Alexander, Kathy. *Paradise Found: The Settlement of the Santa Catalina Mountains.* Mount Lemmon, Ariz.: Skunkworks Productions, 1991.
An excellent account of the "people history" of the Santa Catalina Mountains.

Bowden, Charles. *Frog Mountain Blues.* Tucson: The University of Arizona Press, 1987.
The Tohono O'odham Indians call the Santa Catalinas "Frog Mountain." In this essay the author warns that this unique wilderness can be lost if it becomes too available to man.

Bowers, Janice. *The Mountains Next Door.* Tucson: The University of Arizona Press, 1991.
Bowers writes beautifully of the Rincon Mountains, Tucson's last wilderness.

Burgess, Tony L., and Martha Ames Burgess. "Clouds, Spires and Spines," in *Tucson.* Tucson: Southwestern Mission Research Center, 1986.
An essay about the past, present, and future of the Tucson area.

Cowgill, Pete, and Eber Glendening. *Trail Guide to the Santa Catalina Mountains.* Tucson: Rainbow Expeditions, 1987.
An excellent guide to the trails of the Santa Catalina Mountains.

Gustafson, A. M., ed. *John Spring's Arizona.* Tucson: The University of Arizona Press, 1966.
A series of articles written by John Spring, a teacher and soldier in the Arizona Territory in the 1870s.

Hanson, Roseann Beggy and Jonathan. *Southern Arizona Nature Almanac: A Seasonal Guide to Pima County and Beyond.* Boulder: Pruett Publishing Company, 1996.

Lazaroff, David. *Sabino Canyon: Life of a Southwestern Oasis.* Tucson: The University of Arizona Press, 1993.

Nabhan, Gary Paul. *Saguaro: A View of Saguaro National Monument and the Tucson Basin.* Tucson: Southwest Parks and Monuments Association, 1986.
A collection of essays about the Saguaro National Monument with particular emphasis on the Rincon Mountain Unit.

Olin, George. *House in the Sun.* Tucson: Southwest Parks and Monuments Association, 1977.
A complete narrative about the plants and animals living in the Sonoran Desert as well as an explanation of the desert environment.

Sonnichsen, C. L. *Tucson, the Life and Times of an American City.* Norman: The University of Oklahoma Press, 1982.
Sonnichsen's folksy writing makes the history of Tucson seem like a novel.

Index

Betty Leavengood has lived in Tucson since 1969. As a freelance writer, Betty specializes in local history and travel articles. She especially enjoys keeping the Tucson Hiking Guide *current* by re-hiking the trails. "I'm always trying to figure out how to answer the question I get at book-signings—'Which trail is your favorite?'" she says. "I just can't decide!"